Railroading Around the World

Books by S. Kip Farrington, Jr.

FISHING THE PACIFIC: Offshore and On
FISHING THE ATLANTIC: Offshore and On
PACIFIC GAME FISHING
SPORT FISHING BOATS
A BOOK OF FISHES
ATLANTIC GAME FISHING
THE DUCKS CAME BACK
SHIPS OF THE U. S. MERCHANT MARINE
INTERESTING BIRDS OF OUR COUNTRY
GIANTS OF THE RAILS
RAILROADING FROM THE HEAD END
RAILROADING FROM THE REAR END
RAILROADS AT WAR
RAILROADS OF TODAY
RAILROADING THE MODERN WAY
RAILROADING AROUND THE WORLD

Juvenile
BILL, THE BROADBILL SWORDFISH

Frontispiece. Central Railway of Peru #6 descending grade in the high Andes of Peru.

RAILROADING
AROUND
THE WORLD

by S. Kip Farrington, Jr.

Castle Books   New York

To
E. ROLAND HARRIMAN
businessman, sportsman and railroader, who performs a fine job for the railroad industry as Chairman of the Board of Directors of the Union Pacific Railroad.

Foreword

ON Thursday, May 18, 1950, I made a speech to the New York Railroad Club entitled "Railroading Around the World." I announced to this sizable group of good railroaders that evening that the name of this speech would be the title of a book I would undertake to write. Now some five years later, which isn't too long a time for such an undertaking, the book has appeared, and I trust it will be well received—at least for its pictures if for no other reason.

My principal aim in writing this book was to put before the eyes of the North American railroad men and those interested in U. S. and Canadian operations the job that is being done by railroaders in other parts of the world. The men that I have met, from officials to switchtenders, are all good railroaders who are doing the best possible job with what they have at their disposal, which is all one can ask of anybody. It is this thought that I try to convey in this volume. The United States and Canada are omitted for obvious reasons. I have written six books on the U. S. railroads and two more are scheduled to be written. The Canadian operations are so similar to the U. S. operations that I did not feel Canada had a place in this book, which already contains more pictures than any other railroad book ever done. Among the pictures are many fine ones, which my books always seem fortunate enough to have.

I am particularly indebted to W. W. Stewart, the great railroad photographer, of Auckland, New Zealand, for his pictures which I have used in the New Zealand section; to all of the foreign railroads, officials and railroaders, who showed me over their systems and gave me such great welcome and fine hospitality; to Olive B. Flannery, whose incessant work got the manuscript out in its usual rush; to Dave Edwards of East Hampton, Long Island, who provided the end-paper illustrations and took the pictures of the tablets and staffs, as well as the passes, in the book; and last, but not least, to my new Dictaphone Timemaster, without which there would have been no book. This is the eighth book I have done on this machine, and the new model is even better than its predecessors.

A book that should be in the hands of all who are interested in railways, both around the world and in the United States, is *World Railways,* published at 25 Gilbert Street, London, England, and distributed by Rand McNally in the United States. This volume has been published twice and contains many pictures of motive power and cars, as well as maps and statistics that all enthusiasts would enjoy. The book is a companion to Jane's *Fighting Ships* and *All the World's*

Aircraft, and its accuracy has been brought home to me in comparing its statistics with those given me by the foreign railroads.

The Railway Age magazine is read by railroad men throughout the world and there are few, if any, offices in which I have failed to see a weekly copy. The English *Railway Gazette* is also much in demand outside of North America.

I have tried to keep this book in U.S. pounds and miles as much as possible but there are times when the weights and measures of the countries involved had to be used. I am therefore listing the following metric system figures:

1 kilometer	0.62137 miles
1 metric ton	2,204.6 pounds or 1,000 kilograms
1 ton-kilometer	1 metric ton transported over a distance of 1 kilometer—the metric counterpart of the ton-mile
1 meter	39.37 inches or 3.28 feet

S. KIP FARRINGTON, JR.

Finning Out
East Hampton, Long Island, New York, U.S.A.

Contents

Railroading Around the World

Ecuador

THE Guayaquil and Quito Railway Company was originally an American company built by Archer and John Harmon and E. Hope Norton of the United States. It was nationalized in 1944. It operates 281 miles of railroad between Guayaquil, the chief seaport of Ecuador, and Quito, the capital. Its gauge is 3 feet 6 inches.

The line climbs 9,651 feet in only 49 miles, and amazingly enough with only one switchback. The maximum grade is 5.5 per cent but there are many miles of 4.0 and 4.5 per cent. It reaches a maximum altitude of 11,841 feet before crossing the Quito Plateau, which is 9,375 feet above sea level.

The author was run special on his first trip over this fine railroad by Louis Cordevez, its former president, and has made several trips in passenger and freight service. He considers it one of the six most interesting operations that he has ever ridden and one of the big four in South America. It should be a "must" for every North American interested in railroads. Franklin Ruiz, a great Ecuadorian railroader, is General Manager of this road. He had put in two years on the New York Central, obtaining some North American operational experience.

Quito-bound first-class passenger train on the Guayaquil and Quito, entering the switchback as it climbs the Devil's Nose.

Work train of the Guayaquil and Quito with Baldwin-built 2-8-0 type locomotive (41 of which are in service on this railroad) spreading ballast. The great Chimborazo Volcano is in the background. The line circles this wonderful mountain many times, and the author remembers it as one of the most interesting and beautiful railroad trips he has ever made. He rode these little consolidations around it at an altitude of more than 11,000 feet.

Typical mixed or second-class train on the Guayaquil and Quito Railway leaving the narrows of the Devil's Nose. Maximum curvature is 29 degrees. The standard rail is 55 to 70 pounds per yard.

Baldwin-built 2-8-0 type locomotive with oil train leaving Rio-bamba, division point between Guayaquil and Quito on the fine Ecuadorian road of that name. This road is operated with complete United States practices, and is one of two the author has encountered, throughout the world, where train orders are used.

Peru

ONE of the most spectacular railroads in all the world is the Central Railway of Peru. It is the road that goes to the highest spot in the world for standard gauge—an altitude of 15,865 feet. In fact, there is only one other railroad higher, a small narrow-gauge railroad in Chile. For the altitude and the difficulties connected with construction and maintenance, the Central of Peru without any doubt stands above all the railroads in the world. The highest point is reached at La Cima ("The Summit"), situated on the Morococha Branch 2.1 kilometers from Ticlio, which is on the main line.

The highest point on the main line itself is a short distance from Ticlio, nearly in the center of the Galera Tunnel. The elevation in the tunnel is 15,693 feet. From here the water flows into both the Atlantic and the Pacific Oceans. To reach this altitude the regular passenger and freight trains pass over 41 bridges, through 61 tunnels, and over 13 switchbacks. (They call these switchbacks "zigzags" in Peru.) The running time from the city of Lima is 6 hours and 35 minutes, an average rise of 40 feet per minute being obtained for the 160 kilometers. The total length of the railway including its branches is 416 kilometers or 258 miles, and comprises the system of 40 stations, 58 bridges, 66 tunnels, and 21 switchbacks.

Some 18,000 men were employed during the early days in the construction of the line. The loss of lives through accidents was very heavy.

To describe this railroad, it seems to me that it is just about like railroading up and down the sides of the Grand Canyon of the Colorado River in Arizona.

The author has spent days on this property riding locomotives, business cars, autocarrils, handcars, and has driven in an automobile along the highway which follows it all the way.

The road is operated by Hubert Booker, O.B.E., G.M., and the Traffic Officers, which correspond to our Operational Officers, are Chester Crofton Atkins, Traffic Manager A.G.M., and Edward Charles Guilding, Assistant T.M.

The road has four business cars with rear ends just like the United States official business cars. The Central is dispatched with complete American practices by timetable and United States train orders.

The road owns 300 cars for freight service and every car is made of steel. The heaviest grade is only 4.5 per cent and the average about 3.75 per cent. The entire railroad is uncompensated. The main line is completely rock ballasted and the rail is 70 to 80 pounds per yard. The sharpest curves are 17.5 degrees. For motive power on both freight and passenger service this road uses fine 2-8-0 type oil burners that are on so many roads with sharp curves and are found to curve so readily. They were built in the United States and Great Britain and will handle a maximum of 190 tons up this grade, usually about 4 cars. The road also has 5 Garretts which have been disposed of or are in storage. Their new passenger equipment is excellent, lightweight steel, and fine meals are served en route. Passenger operations are only in the daytime because of the rocks and slides, and the passenger trains coming down the mountain are all preceded by hand cars in case any rocks or slides are encountered.

A trip to Peru, only nine hours from Miami via Pan American Grace Airways and a short trip by air from Europe, is well worth while. Along with operations in Ecuador and Chile, this Peruvian operation should be seen and observed by all.

The Peruvian Corporation, whose head office is in London, England, controls six railroads in Peru, the Central being the most noted, but following it is the Southern Railway of Peru, another great and spectacular operation. The Southern Railway operates from the port of Mollendo to the lake port of Puno on Lake Titicaca, the largest navigable body of water in the world which is 12,500 feet above sea level. Here the freight and passengers are ferried to Guaqui, Bolivia, where it is only a 75 kilometer run to the interesting capital, La Paz, which is reached by the Guaqui–La Paz Railway. This road is also most interesting.

The Peruvian Southern climbs from sea level to Crucero Alto, 14,668 feet in 220 kilometers. Crucero Alto is a little over 100 kilometers from Arequipa, 7,530 feet high, and is only a few hours flying distance from Lima, should anyone interested in looking the railroad over wish to ride it out of there. This road also uses consolidation-type locomotives in passenger and freight service. It has 4 foot 8.5 inch standard gauge, and a total length of 535 miles, or 861 kilometers. Its rail is 70 pounds per yard. Its maximum grade is only 4 per cent and its maximum curvature 17.5 degrees. It has a total of 60-odd passenger cars and 500 to be used in freight service. This is the road that takes you to the famous Cuzco Ruins, which until the salt water fishing became the world's best off Cabo Blanco, in the northern part of this grand country, was Peru's greatest and best-known tourist attraction as well as one of the first places to visit.

The top of the railroad world, Ticlio, with an elevation of 15,800 feet. There is always snow on the beautiful Peruvian Andes.

The Morococha mining camp of the Cerro de Pasco Copper Co. at an elevation of 13,000 feet. The Central of Peru hauls all the copper for Cerro de Pasco and the Vanadium Corporation of America to the port of Callao to be shipped to world ports, and hauls foodstuffs, oil, building materials, and other commodities up the long hard pull to the mines.

A southbound extra coming down the Viso double switchback.

The Casapalca mining camp and yard. Notice the rail inspection auto car at the station platform.

Kilometer 170, 15,000 feet in the Peruvian sky near La Cima. Notice the beautifully ballasted track and good clearance that this railroad has on its entire line.

Chicla Station Terminal and switchback.

Extra 211 north takes water at Huaro, 242 kilometers from Callao, as you can see on the side of the station, amid the beautiful and fertile Huancayo Valley after cresting the divide over the Andes. This is kilometer 313. Notice the rail inspection car on the passing track on the left side of the locomotive, partially hidden by steam from the cylinder cocks.

This is the locomotive that does the trick—one of the latest of the consolidation Class 200 built by Beyer Peacock in England. They have a tractive effort of 36,600 pounds. They also have straight air brakes as well as conventional automatic air brakes. Notice the exceedingly large sand domes and the llama over the first C on the tender. This interesting Peruvian animal is the standard-bearer of the road.

Note how they ride the tops on the Central of Peru. Here the rear-end man has no comfortable caboose or way car, for this extra tonnage could not be handled on these mountain railroads. The train is a northward extra in the Huancayo Valley. Note the steel boxcar of modern construction in the foreground, the two classes of tank cars and the two hoppers on the rear end. The tonnage has been filled out after cresting the summit.

We are getting down now—the elevation is only 14,000 feet at kilometer 159 in the Chunchan Valley as the morning and afternoon crack passenger trains from Callao-Lima and Huancayo make their daily meet right on time.

Southbound passenger train #6 crossing one of the many fine steel bridges on the Central of Peru. This one is over the Camion River.

Chile

THE author has had the interesting experience of riding the Chilean State Railways from one end to the other of this long and narrow country—the longest and narrowest in the world. From Puerto Montt, way at the south, to Valparaiso, the railroad is called the Southern Network or Red Sur. From La Calera, near Valparaiso, the Northern Network or Red Norte begins. The Southern Network has a 5 foot 6 inch gauge and the Northern, 3 foot 3 inch, extending northward all the way to Arica, the topmost port of Chile. The Southern Network is 1,728 miles long and the Northern Network, 963 miles. At Arica, the Arica–La Paz Railroad begins and the Chilean section has grades up to 6 per cent with 26 miles of rack, has 3 foot 3 inch gauge, and 129 miles of operation in Chile.

The fourth section and probably one of the three most interesting in all the world the author has been on and one that everyone should see and ride is the Chilean Transandine, which starts at Los Andes, about 60 kilometers from Santiago. The entire line from Los Andes to Los Cuevas, just past the frontier and through the International Tunnel, is electrified. Los Cuevas has been named "Villa Eva Perón" by the Argentines and now goes under that name. Before the line was electrified from Los Andes to Rio Blanco, the train used to be pulled by a steam engine running backward so that it would not have to be turned in Rio Blanco where the locomotive waited for the opposing train, usually met around Portillo, three-quarters of the way up the grade.

In the first 15 kilometers from Los Andes to Vilcuya, the grade varies from 1.5 to 2.5 per cent, and from Vilcuya to Rio Blanco it is a straight 2.5 per cent. Starting right out of Rio Blanco where the rack railroad begins, it is 8 per cent, then keeps steadily at 7 per cent to Portillo 50 kilometers away, and then goes back to 6.8 per cent almost all the way to the top.

The sharpest curve on the Transandine Line is 100 meters, which is a 15.5 degree curve. There are 27 kilometers of 75 pound rail and 30 kilometers of 60 pound rail; 23 kilometers of rack railroad in all. There are 27 tunnels plus the International Tunnel at the top, which by coincidence is the same length as the altitude, 9,338 feet, which is not very high considering the surrounding heights and how they have to be crossed. You have to give credit to the Clark Brothers who built this railroad. They have a station named after them, Hermanos Clark, and a monument to them just before reaching Portillo. Portillo is probably the world's greatest ski place and is in use, of course, all through the North American summer, which is the Chilean winter. There is a fine hotel there and skiers are brought up on the railroad after they have skied down to many points. There is also a fine lift.

On going by rail you leave Santiago at 7:30 in the morning on the Valparaiso train and the Argentine cars are cut out at Las Vegas, two hours from Santiago. You go through customs at Los Andes. The gauge is 3 feet on the big hill. They use Brown Boveri electric engines built in Switzerland in 1925. Brown Boveri is supposed to turn out the finest rack engines in the world. The Argentines take over at Villa Eva Perón and there are some 10 kilometers of 6 per cent rack, 8 kilometers of 5.5 per cent rack, and about 5 kilometers of 4 per cent rack on the east side. Here the trains are handled by the small Garrett oil-burning locomotives.

Some years, of course, they have great snow difficulties on this railroad but normally they do not encounter snows of much more than 10 feet. There are 27 snowsheds in addition to the tunnels.

Originally the highway, which, as everywhere else, goes along the railroad, was run through the International Tunnel right over the tracks, and all the automobiles were permitted to go through it. But the railroads finally got wise, and get much more business by sending the highway up 15,000 feet and getting it off their right-of-way. There is a wonderful view of Aconcagua, which is the highest mountain in North or South America, 21,900 feet, as you go down the east side. You cannot, however, see the Christ of the Andes Monument, which is a wonderful sight, but you do see it when you fly through on Pan American Grace Airways. The plane follows the railroad all the way through Cumbres Pass, no doubt the most beautiful flight in all the world. The writer has flown through every pass across the Andes south of La Paz, Bolivia, and through all of them in Chile, and, of course, they are all breathtaking. I have also flown around and around Aconcagua. There is snow all through their summer months.

Chile covers about 286,000 square miles and extends for 2,600 miles along the Pacific Ocean. Chile has an average width of 108 miles, 220 miles in width at its widest and 9 miles at its narrowest. Therefore it is definitely a north and south railroad operation. The Southern Railroad has 526 steam locomotives, 669 passenger cars, and 7000 freight cars. They are very up-to-date and employ many U. S. practices. Almost all of their freight cars are steel and when they complete their program for modernizing their passenger equipment, they will be very well set. All cars have automatic couplers. In fact, I think the Chilean State Railways is about as good a railroad as I have ever been on outside of the United States and they railroad better than anywhere else. Chileans are extraordinarily fine railroaders, and that goes for the big roads as well as the small mining roads, several of which I have been on. This is the only railroad outside of the United States where the engine crews call signals, one of the few where they use the train air signal, and the only one I have ever been on where the engine crews are constantly looking back along the train. They have a very fine diesel streamline train which makes the round trip daily from Puerto Montt through the trout country in the south of Chile to Santiago; they call it the Flecha. Their busiest line is between Santiago and Valparaiso, the largest seaport to their largest city and capital. It is double track, electrified all the way and has complete automatic block system with color light signals, and the dispatching is conducted from tower to tower. The line runs from Santiago to Valparaiso across the coast range at La Cumbre and the grade is 2.5 per cent in both directions. The Chileans, of course, just take this in stride; their wonderful new electric engines built by Baldwin-Westinghouse, and Alco–General Electric, using 3,000 volts, can each take 600 tons up the grade with ease. They also have fine electric freight engines. This run reminds one of southern California; in fact, it is like a glorified California all the way except that it is 50 per cent better and you don't have a rattlesnake staring you in the face every time you go out shooting. Chile is no doubt the greatest sporting country of them all with its wonderful salt water fishing and the world's best trout fishing, its superb dove and Perdix shooting, plus the many birds to be seen, and the skiing. As you drop down toward Valparaiso from La Calera, the junction for the line north, you come to the beautiful Pacific with its lovely watering place where the Chileans spend their summer, Viña del Mar, then go along the ocean to Valparaiso, which they call "Puerto," meaning "port." You would be surprised at the number of train movements, freight and passenger, plus the commuting service on either end between Santiago and Llay Llay, 91 kilometers, and from Puerto to San Pedro, 49 kilometers.

The Union Switch and Signal Company has installed all of this road's fine automatic signal system. They have excellent officials, an excellent signal engineer, and believe it or not, have in their Alameda yard the only retarder yard I have seen outside of North America, Switzerland, France and Japan. The Union Switch and Signal Company also installed this. That is really railroading in such a far-off country.

The Chileans use crushed stone and gravel for their ballast, and on the railroad from Santiago to Puerto Montt have no grades over 2 per cent and no curves worse than 10 degrees. They have very fine clearances and the majority of their freight haul is composed of minerals, forest products, and products of agriculture and manufacturing.

On the standard gauge lines most of the rails weigh from 90 to 101 pounds. On the Northern Network with its 3 foot 3 inch gauge they weigh 60 pounds.

The Chileans have excellent steam locomotives as well as electric and they have two classes of mountain-type locomotives built in the United States. The latest one has a tractive effort of 56,750 pounds, with 235 pounds boiler pressure and 66 inch driving wheels. They also have some Mikados and Pacific-type steam engines.

Other railroads I have ridden in Chile are the Ferrocarril Mineral de Chuquicamata, which is operated by the Chile Exploration Company, to the biggest copper mine in the world with standard gauge and 25 electric locomotives; this company is owned by the Anaconda Copper Company of the United States. Also the Cruz Grande–El Tofo, which hauls the ore from the mines at El Tofo to the port of Cruz Grande, where it is brought north in the great ore ships. A subsidiary of Bethlehem Steel, this railroad is also standard gauge and is electrified for 16 miles. The Nitrate Railway at Iquique, Chile, called the Ferrocarril Salitrero de Tarapacá, is also standard gauge and has a length of 348 miles with 59 locomotives, 58 cars. I have spent much time on this and when you pull up over the beautiful port of Iquique, the Palm Beach of Chile, where all the salt water fishing takes place, it is a place always to remember. The Rancagua–El Teniente Railway, operated by the Braden Copper Company, a subsidiary of Kennecot Copper of the United States, has a 2 foot 6 inch gauge, is 45 miles in length, and with 18 steam locomotives carries ore from some of the wonderful Chilean mines. Other nitrate roads are the Mina María Elena, owned by the Anglo-Chilean Nitrate Company, and the Pedro de Valdivia Railway, which also hauls the nitrate on the pampa. These two roads are both 3 foot 6 inch gauge, operate about 90 miles of track, and are electrified.

However, last but not least, the first fine road on which I ever had a pass honored me is the Ferrocarril Tocopilla a El Toco, which takes nitrate from the mines at Pedro de Valdivia and María Elena down to the port of Tocopilla, where before the war we did all our fishing. Tocopilla gave Chile its name as the world's finest swordfishing place. It is 100 miles south of Iquique, where the fishing is now carried on. The El Toco Road has 194 miles of road and 24 miles of it is electrified. They have 39 steam locomotives and 7 electric engines, and I have ridden the road in their business car, which is most interesting, serves an excellent meal with fine porter, but is no bigger than a U.S. caboose. There is one switchback and the grade is 4 per cent dropping down the coastal cordillerra to the port. They bring 18 loaded cars of nitrate down and take 18 to 20 empties up. As usual, they do not use cabooses and it is a spectacular sight to see the Chilean brakemen riding the tops of the cars as they do in Peru, with the mufflers they always wear flying in the breeze.

Autocarril operated special for the author makes a stop between Portillo and the International Tunnel at Frontera, which is half on the Chilean side and half on the Argentine, so that pictures may be taken of the rack railroad for this book. Note the rack in the center of the track. This is a typical type of Chilean snow shed. The author is just putting his notebook in his pocket while chief signal engineer Evans and Mrs. Farrington stand in the background. This is typical of the country through which the railroad operates.

This photograph shows the monument erected in memory of the "Brothers Clark," who built the Transandine Railway. Standing from left to right in front of the monument are Geoffrey Evans, chief signal engineer in charge of construction of the Chilean State railways; Mrs. Farrington; Raymond Reyes, chief of the tariff division, who has been in the United States many times inspecting its railroads; Al Heany, United States diplomat in Chile; the chief engineer of the Transandine Railway; and the Pan American-Grace Airways photographer.

One of the few photographs ever taken by the author in all his travels. This shot was snapped from the cab of the electric locomotive hauling the International train up the 8 per cent section of the rack railroad, looking up to one of the tunnels on the 7.7 section. This gives a small idea of the way the line is built, the grades, and the rough and tough country it traverses.

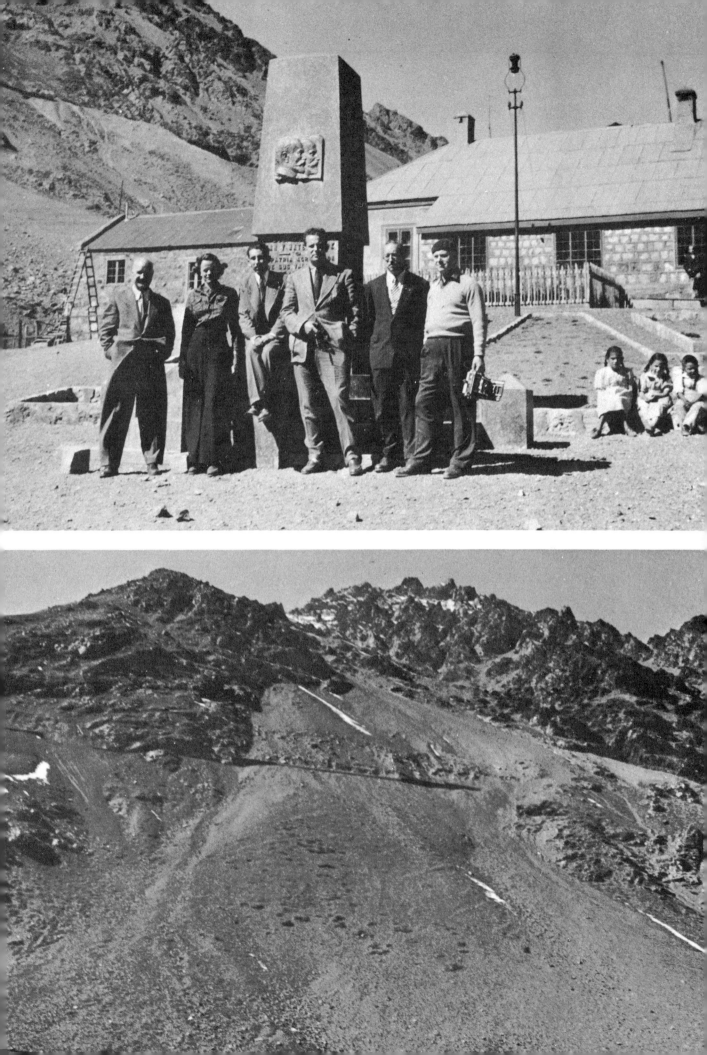

Picturesque scene with horse-drawn sled for the skiers in the foreground at the Portillo Station, Chile's great skiing place 9,000 feet up in the high Andes. The train is a skier's special which has just arrived from Santiago. Many ski specials are, of course, operated in Chile as in the United States and Switzerland during the winter months.

The author has just arrived at Mapocho Station in Santiago from Valparaiso on this fine electric engine which has been spotted to allow this photograph to be made of the then (1950) heads of the Chilean State Railways, both operational and traffic, greeting the author. Note the *maquinista*—Spanish for "engineer" —doffing his elaborate cap in the cab. These are fine engines and are operating on a railroad where *Vía libre*, which means "the line is clear," is constantly called.

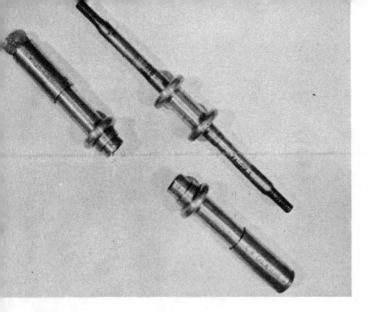
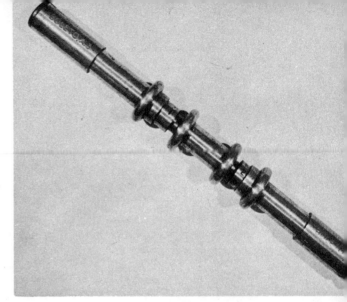

A staff used on the Chilean State Railways, typical of those in use in staff systems around the world. The Spaniards call them *boletos*. You can see the number on the staff. It can be disconnected and used for one, two, or three sections of a train and, of course, no train can pass any point where the staff is delivered and received without having the staff for the next staff section of the railroad. The Chileans pick their staffs up at faster speed than I have ever seen in any other country. Their diesel streamlined trains on the main line south from Santiago to Puerto Montt pick them up and deliver them in miniature mail cranes at a good 50 miles per hour and it is rare that they ever miss.

In districts where they do not have the automatic pick-up and delivery, the fireman puts on a long leather glove heavily padded so that the hook will not hurt his arm as he picks the staff out from another type of catch and deliver mechanism which would correspond to one of our mail cranes. This is one of the most unique gloves that I have ever seen.

Pass presented to Mr. and Mrs. S. Kip Farrington, Jr., by the Chilean State Railways on their first trip over the system, shown both closed and in open position. Note the authorization to ride the locomotives stamped in the upper left-hand corner. The foreign roads would not think of having an American railroad writer, or any other official, on their property without presenting them with a pass. Their hospitality is beyond belief.

utorizado pars
RM. T 1
la..... zomotoras
Año 1950
Traccion y Mixr.s.

F. CC. DEL ESTADO
CHILE
—

ASE LIBRE
ODAS LAS LINEAS
INCLUSO
F. C. TRANSANDINO
PRIMERA CLASE
CON DERECHO A CAMA
Y PULLMAN.

N.º A. 16.—

Sr. S. Kip Farrington
Jr. y señora

DIRECTOR GENERAL

La Dirección no se responsabiliza por ningún perjuicio que pueda sufrir el tenedor de este pase, en sus viajes.

S. Kip Farrington

FIRMA DEL INTERESADO

1950

FERROCARRI

DEL ESTAD

Bolivia

THE railroads of Bolivia are included with Chile because of the interchange and the fact that two of the main ports, Arica and Antofagasta, Chile, are open ports for Bolivia, as well as Mollendo in Peru, which was described in the Peruvian section of this book. As already stated, the Arica Road in Chile is a 6 per cent rack road which goes on to La Paz, the Bolivian capital. But the most interesting operation is that of the Antofagasta and Bolivia Railway from Antofagasta up to La Paz. The international train is operated three times a week. The distance is 729 miles and takes 31 hours. The train is equipped with good Chilean dormitory cars, as the sleepers are called in many countries, particularly in South America, and they are very comfortable. This road has a few steel and concrete ties but most of the ties, of course, are made of the great Chilean oak, which does not need treating. The maximum curvature on this line is 23 degrees and the heaviest grades are only 3.3 on the main line and 4.1 on the branches.

The road operates some 1,150 miles in Chile and 750 miles in Bolivia. The rail weighs up to 75 pounds per yard and the gauge is 3 feet 3 inches.

From the port of Antofagasta the main line climbs to 1,800 feet in 18 miles. At San Pedro, 197 miles, the line is at 10,630 feet elevation and the highest point on the Chilean section, 13,000 feet, is reached at Ascotan, 227 miles from Antofagasta. The line then drops down to 12,341 feet at the Chile-Bolivia border, 276 miles, and runs along the high plateau at 12,000 feet over the Bolivian tableland before rising to 13,134 feet, the highest on the Bolivian section, 10 miles from La Paz, where it descends to 12,143 feet at the La Paz Station. The narrow gauge branch from Ollagüe to Punto Alto, Chile, 59 miles long, which was built in 1907 to serve the copper mines at Collahuasi, attains a height of 15,909 feet and is the only railroad in the world higher than the Central of Peru, which is, of course, standard gauge. They have some fine new 4-8-2 type locomotives.

Bolivia is a most extraordinary and beautiful country. Flying in at 17,000 feet, to the highest capital in the world, you will also land in the highest airport in the world at 13,000 feet. It is a very interesting experience to stand behind the pilot in the cockpit of a Panagra plane and watch the altimeter go down to only 13,000 feet as you land. You then drop down to the city itself, which is 11,900 feet to 12,143 feet depending upon which part of it you are in. The automobile road itself is on a 7 per cent grade coming down from the airport. To see Bolivia from the air and from the railroad, coming in on its various approaches, is a sight that no one interested in railroads should ever miss.

Pass of the Antofagasta and Bolivia Railway in open and shut positions.

Argentina

AS you can see from the passes illustrated here, the Argentine railroads have been taken over from the French and British owners who formerly operated them and have been named after famous Argentine generals. There are many types of operations in the Argentine, water conditions are bad, and as the engine tanks do not carry much water, frequent stops are made for this important part of steam locomotive operation. A good many of the Argentine roads are electrified out of Buenos Aires. There are various gauges in the Argentine but most of the gauge is 5 feet 6 inches, although there is some standard and also some meter gauge.

There are seven different roads operating in the Republic today. The General San Martin operates the Argentine side of the Transandine Railway and from Mendoza to the summit at Frontera, and has 6 per cent grade with a rack railroad. They are now operating some diesels and new lightweight cars.

Author's pass on General San Martin Railroad in the Argentine. Pictures are required on many South American roads.

MINISTERIO DE TRANSPORTES DE LA NACION

FERROCARRIL NACIONAL GENERAL SAN MARTIN

Ministerio de Transportes de la Nación

F. C. N. Gral. SAN MARTIN
—
PASE LIBRE
PRIMERA CLASE

No. 53

TODAS LAS LINEAS

Con cama para viajar en todos los Trenes sin restricción, Locomotoras, Pullman, con derecho al Transporte de Equipaje.

INTRANSFERIBLE

EXPEDIDO AL
Sr. S. Kip Farrington
ESPECIAL
Válido del 1/1/50 al 31/3/50

GERENTE GENERAL

The grand hall of the station plaza of the General Roca Railway in Buenos Aires.

Brazil

THE Santos and Jundiai ranks as one of the author's "Big Six" in the world's most interesting operations. Although a short railroad—it is only 86 miles in length —it serves the great coffee port of Santos, the city of São Paulo, and connects at Jundiai with the crack Paulista Railroad for Campanas, Bauru and Colombia. The Santos and Jundiai has a gauge of 5 feet 3 inches and the line is electrified between São Paulo and Jundiai, a distance of 40 miles, where the maximum grade is 2.5 per cent.

It also operates extremely fine service with lightweight diesel trains called the Comets between Santos and São Paulo in an hour and a half, including the 30 minutes spent ascending and descending the Serra incline. This road is operated by Dr. Renato Feio, a fine engineer and crack all-around railroader, who would be capable of operating any system in the world. Much new U. S. equipment is in use.

The Serra incline is, without a question, one of the railroading wonders of the world.

The Leopoldina Railroad operates 1,902 miles of 3 foot 3.5 inch gauge in Brazil, the main lines running from Rio de Janeiro to Victoria, Caratinga, Manhuassú, and Petropolis. They also have a big suburban business out of Rio. They have a 14 per cent grade rack railroad to Petropolis and they triple the trains, not double them. It is the heaviest grade I have been on in South America, in fact anywhere in the world except Switzerland.

The Paulista Railroad is a privately owned railroad operating 514 miles of 5 foot 3 inch gauge and 402 miles of 3 foot 3.5 inch gauge, as well as 39 miles of 2 foot gauge. It is beautifully run and operated, electrified for 241 miles on the 5 foot 3 inch section. Like the Jundiai, it has recently installed automatic couplers.

Many of its operating officers attended college in the United States and Dr. Jayme Cintra, its president, is an excellent all-around railroad man and engineer.

The Central Railway of Brazil runs from Rio de Janeiro to São Paulo to Belo Horizonte and other cities and operates 810 miles of 5 foot 3 inch gauge and 1,440 miles of 3 foot 3.5 inch gauge. From Barra to Belo Horizonte the line is equipped with Centralized Traffic Control, Union Switch and Signal Company having supplied the installation and done much work in Brazil. This road boasts 2-10-4, 4-8-4, and 4-8-2 type engines, built recently in the United States, but it has now gone diesel as much as possible and operates through lightweight day trains with fine new Budd equipment and overnight Budd-equipped trains from Rio to São Paulo, the two chief cities of this great country.

Grades up to 2 per cent are encountered after leaving Rio de Janeiro. The suburban service out of São Paulo is big, but the electrified section out of Rio de Janeiro carries an enormous number of people who ride the trains in and out of the city every day.

Two 1,000-horsepower U.S.-built diesels doubleheading crack passenger train near Bauru, between São Paulo and Jundiai. This train is run solid over the Paulista Railroad. This part of the line is now completely electrified.

New 3,000-horsepower 120-metric-ton electric locomotive built in England for the São Paulo–Jundiai electrification. As the Santos and Jundiai prior to 1946 was operated by the British, there are still many of their practices on the railroad, which, however, are being modernized as rapidly as possible.

Freight train approaching siding near the bottom of the Serra incline. Santos Plain is in the background. The engine is practically nothing more than a brake and the tonnage is usually pushed up, with the engine on the head end descending, the cable, of course, doing the real work.

Descending passenger train meets a freight train on viaduct #4 of the new Serra Nova incline.

Engine house and bank head on the Serra Nova incline. Small steam engines, grip cable at every incline, leaving one and taking next at following bank head. Five 1,000-horsepower fixed engines operate endless cables over the 6½ mile 8 per cent grade section.

Tank cars on the Serra Nova. The tonnage is usually reduced to four or five cars. They take 110 tons up the new Serra 8 per cent grade and 90 tons up the old one with its 10 per cent incline. One million metric tons of oil products move yearly from Santos to São Paulo. Dr. Feio had a pipeline put into operation in January, 1952, which relieved the cable section of 1,500,000 gross metric tons, thus making it available for general freight.

Upgrade cut at the left is ready to take second cable and awaits downgrade cut to make complete movement. This is the perfect meet. The engine is taking water. There are no tunnels on the old incline but six on the new one.

The British railroaders call this a three-wheel bogie. It is also called an inspection trolley. Here Ernest Piles, the division superintendent, and J. C. Stewart, chief mechanical engineer, ride it down the 8 per cent grade. It has a clasp brake which is applied by handling a stick which the front man has his hands around. George H. Minchin, retired operating vice president of the Santa Fe, told the author when he gave him the details of his trip on this railroad, "You're a bigger damn fool than I thought you were to be riding such a contraption down 8 and 10 per cent grades." It is light and simple to lift from one track to another over the cable.

Cable gang working at the bottom of the Serra incline. The Santos Plain is in the background, and a yard for reducing tonnage for both inclines is on the right.

Serra Velha engine on the old "tail end" cable incline. There are four such inclines on the five mile 10 per cent grade line. The engines on the new line are very similar.

Serra Nova siding. Trains operating over the three-rail line negotiate the four-rail meeting sections in the center of every incline. Note how the cables are tipped and the well maintained track.

Venezuela

VENEZUELA is a great country and the railroad system comprises ten small roads and six industrial railroads, all government operated. This country is rapidly building new railroads and soon will have a big network serving many of the important cities. The present roads are mostly 3 foot 6 inch gauge with some 2 foot gauge. Venezuela is steadily trying to improve all the roads.

One of the most interesting operations in the world today is that of the Orinoco, a subsidiary of the United States Steel Corporation in Venezuela, which prospected and found the iron-ore deposit at the hill now called "Cerro Bolivar." The Oliver Mining Company, a subsidiary of the U.S. Steel Corporation, sent representatives into the iron ranges of Venezuela, and the result was that, with the kind cooperation of the Venezuelan Government, modern methods of mining were introduced and the United States now receives thousands of tons of ore a year from this wonderful operation which, of course, required a railroad to move the ore to a seaport. The Orinoco Railroad has 560 ore cars carrying 90 tons each, and they are equipped with standard Westinghouse air brakes as well as an additional straight air line—which makes it possible to apply the brakes and charge the air reservoirs at the same time, thus providing an added safety factor. This is the same system as that used on so many mountain roads. It can be adapted here, of course, because there is no interchange of cars. The cars are grouped in the assembly yard at the western end of the hill 1,000 feet above the base line, where they are run down a 3 per cent grade to the Savanna and then continue on downgrade to the port. Nine 1,600-horsepower Baldwin Lima Hamilton diesel-electric locomotives are in service and three of them take 123 loads over the maximum grades on this track which are 0.5 per cent. They are so short as not to be governing. The ruling grade with the equipment described is 0.2 per cent. The maximum curvature on the hill is 12 degrees and on the Savanna 3 degrees. Trains are allowed to run up to 45 miles an hour and the average round trip running time from the hill assembly yard to Puerto Ordáz and return is figured at 7 hours and 50 minutes. The track is standard gauge laid on 12 inches of crushed-stone ballast under a bottom of ties used on all the main lines. The ties are creosoted southern pine and gum from the United States. A smaller number of native ties were used but the soft wood as usual was unsuitable because of the lack of creosoting facilities and slow local production. The rail is 132 pounds per yard. The road also has all complete accessory cars and a 250 ton wrecking crane. The average movement per day is two loaded and two empty trains for an average of 5 million tons per year. The railroad is entirely equipped with Centralized Traffic Control installed by the Union Switch and Signal Company.

There are four long passing tracks that, with CTC, give the railroad very near the capacity of double track. They also have a complete high-frequency radio system between Caracas and Ciudad Bolívar, Puerto Ordáz and Ciudad Pía.

One of the most interesting operations this road performs is the control of heavily loaded ore cars on a 7 mile downgrade averaging 3 per cent from the hill assembly yard to the Savanna. Two runaway tracks are provided in this section with switches set for through-track operation. If the speed of the car exceeds 21 miles per hour during the run through an electrical time section of the road just preceding the location of the runaway track, the switch is automatically thrown and the ore cars will leave the main track to be slowed and stopped by the adverse grade of the runaway track. From the base of Cerro Bolivar to the conditioning plant at Puerto Ordáz the country is a generally rolling savanna with scattering high hills. Its vegetation is sparse and jungle growth is confined to lowlands and the water courses. There are excellent aggregate and fill materials and also plenty of granite for use as ballast. Eight steel bridges were required on the line, all of them small, but three were required for the highways. The ore-handling and storage system at Puerto Ordáz was designed, manufactured and constructed by the Link Belt Company, its associates and sub-contractors.

The car dumper and barney haul are designed to handle 67 90 ton capacity ore cars per hour. The ore-crushing and conveyor system is designed to handle 6,000 long tons per hour with provision to double this rate. The ore storage yard has a storage capacity of 7,000 tons. The car dumper built by the Wellman Engineering Company is probably the most rugged ever built, considering the weight of the loaded ore cars and the fast time cycle. The massive primary gyratory crusher built by Allis-Chalmers is installed in a pit in the line rock 100 feet deep. Other features are the reclaiming tunnels under the stock pile with a continuous slot and rotary plows to feed ore to conveyor belts; a continuous sampling system which takes 60 tons off the belt per hour and reduces this to a 5-pound sample; the avoidance of hoppers and the use of apron feeders to transfer belts to provide more uniform belt loading and better operating characteristics; and the use of a variable direct current voltage system from reclaiming tunnels to ship loaders so as to provide a completely interlocked variable speed operation. The main shops are at Puerto Ordáz.

Yes, this is one of the most interesting ore roads I have been over and reminds me of the fine operations on the Duluth, Mesabi and Iron Range and the Bessemer and Lake Erie—also controlled by the U.S. Steel Corporation. I have not yet been up to Labrador to look at that great operation, but hope to in the near future.

Benjamin Fairless, Chairman of the Board of the U.S. Steel Corporation, in a speech in Caracas struck the perfect note between the United States and South American countries when he said, "The U.S. Steel and Orinoco Mining Company have come to your gracious country, Venezuela, as foreigners but we hope to remain here in this community as welcome residents and as respected neighbors for many years to come."

Mr. Fairless as usual said the right thing.

Orinoco Mining Railroad engine pushing loaded ore cars into the ore dumper at Puerto Ordáz.

Ore cars behind road diesel at the ore-loading platform at Cerro Bolivar.

Classification yards at Puerto Ordáz. Notice the fine track with its excellent ballast, heavy rail, creosoted ties and turnouts.

One car in the ore dumper, other standing by for the barney haul to boost it into the dumper. The dumper is directly over the primary crusher. This is the type of ore car used on this fine operation.

Alaska

THE Alaska Railroad is government owned and operated under the auspices of the Department of the Interior, of which Douglas McKay is Secretary. A good friend of mine, R. N. Whitman, a fine all-around railroader who was superintendent of the Great Northern's Cascade Division before getting the appointment to become general manager of the Alaska Railroad, has his headquarters at Anchorage where the railroad maintains its offices. The road is 539 miles in length, has 37 steam locomotives in operation and 22 diesels. It owns 1,618 freight cars, 35 passenger cars, 8 rail cars, and 981 miscellaneous pieces of equipment. It is standard gauge and its track is beautifully maintained. Its service is getting better and better, despite the tough conditions under which it has to operate.

Streamliner Aurora with majestic Mt. McKinley in the background. This photograph illustrates why this road is called the Mt. McKinley Route, as this mountain is the highest in North America, towering 20,300 feet above sea level.

Three-unit Electro Motive diesel passing Bartlett Glacier, 48 miles north of Seward. The Alaska Railroad carries both military and civilian freight from the deep water ports of Seward and Whittier to the cities and military bases in the interior.

The streamliner Aurora crosses Hurricane Gulch at mile 284. This structure is 918 feet long and 296 feet above the creek. Mt. McKinley is only 46 miles away.

A passenger extra running through the Nenana River Canyon north of Mt. McKinley National Park. The famous Alaskan Dall sheep are seen from the railroad in the vicinity of where this picture was taken.

The great Electro Motive 3-unit 4,500-horsepower diesel in Alaska. This grand piece of modern motive power has sliced hours off freight and passenger schedules on the Alaska Railroad. Passenger runs between Anchorage and Fairbanks, 356 miles of rugged mountains and swampy muskeg, required two days just five years ago in 1950, but the trip is now easily completed in one day.

Switzerland

SWITZERLAND is a wonderful land of lovely views and mountains, fine people, excellent food and hotels, and great service. Its strategic importance in the European picture has been more than well demonstrated in two World Wars. It is a most important stronghold and actually the heart of Europe.

Naturally a country of such importance would be bound to have good railroads and the Swiss can well be proud of their wonderful operations over a rugged terrain. The Swiss Federal Railways can qualify with the best roads anywhere. The headquarters of this fine railway is in Bern and the railroad was nationalized way back in 1898. The road owns 2,807 kilometers of standard gauge and 73 kilometers of narrow gauge. They operate 1,134 kilometers of double track, 2,600 kilometers of electrified line (about 1,700 miles), and 300 kilometers where steam is the motive power. Before we go any farther, it might be well to tell you that one mile is the equal of 1.609 kilometers. The total length of the Swiss Federal Railway including the station, yard, and workshop area is 6,163 kilometers. They have 2,076 bridges between 2 and 10 meters, 343 over 10 meters, and 225 over 30 meters. A meter is 3 feet. In all they have 2,944 bridges with a total length of 38 kilometers. The wonderful four-track bridge at Bern over the Aare River is 3,609 feet long, 43 feet in width, with a maximum span of 492 feet. It is 121 feet above the river. This is the largest four-track bridge in the world. There are 240 tunnels on the system with a total length of 170.2 kilometers. There are 821 stations, with one station for every 3.5 kilometers, and there are 200 branching-off stations, one bifurcation for every 14 kilometers. They have 7,032 crossovers with roads or other railways. Their level crossings or highway crossings number 1,182 and their guarded level crossings 1,092. Can you imagine having to guard that many crossings on one system in the United States? Crossing after crossing is protected by flagmen, even where the density of traffic is amazingly light—perhaps only three or four horse-drawn vehicles a day. There are few automatic gates and wigwags.

The Swiss have 610 fine electric locomotives whereas their steam locomotives are now down to 278, and they have 263 other traction vehicles such as electric railcars, or freight and passenger shunting tractors and automobiles. They have 21,103 goods wagons or freight cars and 3,534 passenger coaches. Their volume of traffic is terrific, as is their density. In 1920 their gross ton per kilometer was 6,305,810,978. In 1951, it had risen to 17,101,774,986. Their train kilometers in 1920 were 23,250,545 and in 1951, 65,410,928. In 1920 they carried 86,080,314 passengers; in 1951, 201,101,000 passengers with a daily average of approximately 560,000 persons who were carried in about 2,000 passenger trains every twenty-four hours. Their train movements per day number around 3,000. Their volume of traffic on some portions of the open line is up to 250 trains and on some stations up to 600 per day. However, North Americans must remember that while Switzerland has wonderful highways there are not anywhere near as many private automobiles, and highways are also subjected to heavy weather conditions in the winter. Therefore, the Swiss railroads have to provide good service for the citizens, and because of the heavy grades they cannot haul trains that are as long as they might be if the railroading were flat. However, there is little duplication of service and the on-time performance is as fine as any country in the world—probably better. In two weeks of consecutive riding on Swiss passenger trains, I never was on any train that was late at any home terminal and on the road I was never more than eight minutes late at any station. And this was in the middle of February with a terrific amount of snow and very cold weather.

One of the most interesting trips I made in Switzerland was from St. Moritz down to Reichenau Tamins on the Rhetian Railway where I connected with another of their trains for Disentis where I would connect with a train of the Furka-Oberalp Railway. This trip across three cantons (counties) at 7,000 or 8,000 feet, in the rural districts in the mountains, was one of the greatest I have ever taken. With 5 or 6 feet of snow it was a pure white world of its own. After arriving at Disentis, I took the Furka-Oberalp train to Andermatt, where we dropped down the 17.9 per cent grade over the top of the Gotthard Tunnel at Göschenen, where I was to make connections for a southbound train to Chiasso, Italy, through the Gotthard Tunnel. I am relating this story to tell you that I never had more than five minutes to make any of these connections, that no train was to be held for the connection, and that this route was lined up for me by the Swiss railroaders on the Rhetian and the Swiss Federal Railways just as nonchalantly as I am telling it in this book. I was on the locomotives that day from 8:00 A.M. to 9:30 P.M., but all these connections were made with the greatest of ease in that type of weather. It speaks well for their railroads.

In 1951 their traffic revenue totaled 715,483,000 francs and their expenses were 501,112,000 francs. This, of course, is in Swiss francs. Their traffic revenues are made up of passenger traffic, 38.5 per cent; goods, luggage, animal and postal traffic, 53.51 per cent; various, 8.14 per cent. They employ 35,023 persons, which is the yearly average divided up as follows: general management, 2.31 per cent; stations and operating staff, 55.38 per cent; permanent way and power stations, 16.58 per cent; motive power and workshops 25.11 per cent; various service, 0.62 per cent.

The gauge of the Swiss Federal Railways is standard, 4 feet 8.5 inches. They only operate one or two narrow gauge lines and their main line rail averages about 92 pounds per yard. Their rail lengths average from 59 to 118 feet and are joined by joint bars and bolts. They use more steel ties than any road I have ever been on—a great many more—and over 70 per cent of their ties are steel, which are laid at 2,540 feet per mile. They have stone ballast. The heaviest grades are only 2.6 per cent and they have no curves worse than 6 degrees, which is astonishing, particularly so when we stop to consider all the other grades around the country. Switzerland has other very well operated roads called the Swiss Light Railways. These take in all the rack and pinion and funicular railways and tramways, all the narrow gauge railways, and all the standard gauge private railways. These light railways have various gauges and are first class systems in themselves. The Lötschberg Railway, which operates the line from Bern to Brig via the Lötschberg Tunnel, the second longest in the world, and connects with the Simplon main line, is a very busy 148 miles of railroad. The Furka-Oberalp Railway is also a terrifically busy one, as is the Rhetian Railway. The author has had the privilege of riding all three of these, and he also rode the Wengernalp Railway, the Bernese Oberland Railway, and the Jungfrau Railway, all of which companies we will speak of later.

There is a great deal of operation with electric locomotives in Switzerland, much more than in any other country I have been in. All the electrified lines have automatic train control which is provided at all starting and distance signals and operates through the dead man's pedal. Audible warning is given to the engineman who passes the signal of danger, but if he has not stopped after his train is 164 to 197 feet beyond such signals the emergency application is automatically made and the main switches are cut out. The manual block system is the one most generally in use on the nonmechanical signal sections of the railroad. These signals are gradually being replaced by multiple-unit cut or light signals, and mechanically operated signal box equipment is being replaced by relay interlocking. Types of mechanical signals now in use are semaphore for stop signals and disk for distance signals, somewhat similar to a position light signal used in the United States. In the back of this book the Swiss railway signals are illustrated.

The importance of the Basle railway system for Swiss and international traffic can not be emphasized enough. Basle, Bâle, or Basel, as it is written in English, French, or German, is situated at the transition between the low and high lands and is a historical crossroad on the highways of nations, with a unique political situation close to the frontiers of three countries. Beside being the present terminus for the navigation on the Rhine, it is an intersection point for practically all European railway lines, and fast trains, from all directions, exchange their passengers at this center.

After the opening of the Gotthard Railway in 1882 and, two years later, of the Arlberg Railway, Basle became the point of intersection between the important central line from north to south and another, avoiding Germany, from west to east. Here the railway network connects up with Rhine navigation to Rotterdam, Amsterdam, and Antwerp, and therefore with the ocean.

Basle may be considered as a kind of clearing office for European goods traffic, especially suitable for collective shipments to the Scandinavian countries and England, as well as to the ports of the North Sea, the Atlantic Ocean, the Mediterranean, and the Adriatic Sea. Custom-controlled warehouses and efficient cold storage facilities are also provided. Basle is furthermore a center for international fairs. It is, therefore, no coincidence that many great forwarding agencies have their head offices in Basle.

In order to deal with this necessarily heavy traffic, there is, to start with, the railway system known under the name of Basle SBB or Basle SFR (Swiss Federal Railways), separated into a passenger station, goods station, and a marshalling yard. There is furthermore a separate layout for goods traffic, by the name of St. Johann. All these, though owned by the Swiss Federal Railways, are considered international joint stations. The "Badischer Bahnhof," or Basle German Station, with a very extensive railway system, is situated on the other side of the Rhine.

It is necessary, in order to complete the picture, to mention also the three harbor stations on the river Rhine, namely Kleinhuningen, St. Johann, and Birsfelden. Their wharves reach a length of nearly 5 kilometers, their railway lines 64 kilometers, and they have 40 special installations for transshipment purposes, as well as 16 grain elevators and warehouses, the latter with a total capacity of 220,000 tons.

Of all goods imported into Switzerland, more than two-thirds enter at Basle, somewhat more than one-third by waterway and another third by the right and left Rhenish railway lines; the remainder, less than one-third of all Swiss imports, is divided among all the other frontier stations.

In the passenger traffic, Basle station is responsible for 6 per cent of the total receipts, second only to Zurich's main station, whereas in the goods traffic, it is, together with the Rhine harbors, with 16 per cent of the total takings, far above all the other Swiss stations.

In international traffic Basle has to deal daily with direct fast train services to Paris, to Luxembourg, Belgium, Holland, and the Channel ports (England). In fact Basle is reached by the greatest number of through coaches of any station in Europe.

In 1951, a daily average of 538 trains left or entered the Basle area; i.e., 254 passenger and 284 goods trains.

The total track included in the layout of the Basle railway system reaches a length of 262 kilometers, or 164 miles.

All these details should give an outline of the importance of Basle as the main entrance to Switzerland and as an international thoroughfare, illustrating at the same time the many-sided operating tasks involved.

The Marshalling Yard of Basle SFR

The station premises and plant of Basle have, in general, been gradually developed from a rather primitive state up to the present standard in accordance with the increase of traffic. As far as the plant and installations for goods traffic are concerned, their development was influenced especially by the heavy traffic increases shortly after the First World War, concurrent with the extension of navigation on the Rhine as far as Basle, and the creation of new harbor facilities. The extra shunting space needed and, therefore, the creation of a new marshalling yard in the Muttenz area, was, however, also due to the application of new principles and the introduction of new methods in goods conveyance. These new methods consisted mainly in the reorganization of goods traffic in such a way as to eliminate shunting operations at intermediate stations and to concentrate such work, as far as possible, at important marshalling yards. In these yards trains had to be formed so that they would be able to run through to the next terminal station with a minimum of shunting in between, thereby speeding up the wagon circulation and reducing the time required for goods conveyance as well as saving shunting expenditure.

The arrival line-group "A" consists of as many as 13 lines. This number is necessary because of the trains arriving from neighboring countries and having to go through the customs examination. Without sufficient space the rolling stock detained by this examination might overflow and block up the approach lines.

From the line-group "A" the trains are shunted over the double-incline into the 43 lines of the redirection line-group "B." The long-distance-goods trains having been assembled here and needing no further shunting are advanced into the departure line-group "D," ready to leave when the time arrives. The line-group "B" also has lines provided for wagons remaining at the disposal of the consignee, who has still to indicate their final destination. Once this is known they have as a rule to be dealt with on the double-incline a second time.

Beside the main line-groups, already dealt with, the station contains the following plant and installations:

The Customs Group "J." This line-group deals with wagons requiring detailed customs examination. They are for such purpose collected in a special line of line-group "B," hauled to the customs-group "J," and return, after examination, across the double-incline to where they have to be sorted out. The layout is completed by a wagon repair plant "R," locomotive sector "T," and the transshipping plant "U."

In view of the length of the direction lines (up to 830 meters, or more than half a mile), an efficient double-incline is of primary importance; its heights must enable the wagons to run through the distribution area even under the most unfavorable conditions. A "summer-hump" at lesser height is, therefore, provided for normal working and a higher "winter-hump" for periods which are not favorable to easy running.

Regarding the actual work carried out in this important marshalling yard, there are, of course, a number of other items which, even in this short outline, must be mentioned. For instance:

1. The regulation of the running speed, off the double-incline, of each individual wagon, according to requirements, by means of rail brakes.

2. The special considerations needed, depending on whether wagons are loaded or empty, whether they require special care, whether they are to be treated singly or in groups, and, of course, where they have to be dispatched to.

3. The centralized signaling and safety plant necessary for such a widely ramified layout, which includes electrically interlocked block order and signalman's cabins as well as motor-driven points and signals.

4. Semiautomatic, double-incline layout affecting all points for the sorting out of wagons for line-group "B" with fast-action switch-levers (throw-over within 0.6 seconds).

5. Double-incline light signals indicating "stop," "slow-pushing," and "fast-pushing."

6. Auxiliary locking frame "III" on the double-incline to be used in case of disturbances in the automatic switch operating mechanism.

7. Loudspeakers for communications between the shunting master and signalman, as well as a pneumatic post for the conveyance of written instructions.

8. Signal cabin IV (perhaps the most interesting part of the yard), with its desk-form switch-control installation, allows such a presetting for automatic switch-point operation, according to a definite sorting-out schedule, that all points turn automatically, as required, after a wagon or group of wagons has passed them. After the signalman has duly set all the levers (up to 50) controlling the automatic operation of all points, in accordance with the schedule in front of him, the train pushed over the double-incline is sorting itself out, so to speak, of its own accord, but for the help of rail brakes and scotch blocks operated by the shunting staff. No switch-point needs attention after the operation has started.

The marshalling yard of Basle-Muttenz, in its present not yet completed form, with a length of 4 kilometers, or 2½ miles, including 84 kilometers, or 52½ miles, of track and 222 switch-points, is the largest of its kind in Switzerland. It deals with the daily splitting up of 70 arriving trains with approximately 3,000 wagons and forms again nearly as many.

Preliminary plans and studies are being made in order to find out the most suitable way to carry out the proposed second stage of construction. The question as to whether its extension should consist of a double layout, with separate up and down shunting areas, or in a simple widening of the present yard has yet to be decided upon. Whatever the solution may be, it must be a yard worthy of the outstanding importance of the goods traffic it has to deal with.

The Gotthard Line

The Swiss Railway officials and employees are very proud of their Gotthard Line and they truly should be. Like the wonderful Swiss precision watch, it runs and operates well. It provides a direct connection between the north and south of Europe, passing through regions known throughout the world for their great beauty. From all sides branch lines approach points of departure and terminal. In the north it serves England, Ireland, Holland, and Belgium, large parts of France and Germany, as well as Scandinavian countries, Italy, the eastern part of the French Riviera, and certain Adriatic countries in the south. From the frontier station of Basle, fast trains of the Gotthard Line bring the traveler in one hour and a half to Lucerne, passing the Jura Mountains through the five-mile-long Hauenstein Tunnel to the important railway junction at Olten. I made six trips through this tunnel and it is another good one. Between Brunnen and Fluelen, there are 13 tunnels in 11 kilometers, the longest being 3,375 meters. Then the Gotthard Line approaches the three great spiral tunnels on the north side of the Gotthard. The first of the spirals is the Pfaffensprung Tunnel, which is 1,614 yards long. It is entered at 2,539 feet altitude and is left at 2,654 feet. The little church at Wassen is rounded here for the first time at this level. The next tunnel is the Wattinger, 1,185 yards long, which is entered at 2,936 feet altitude and left at 3,012 feet. The line is now even with the church at Wassen and you circle it again as you enter the last of the three spirals at this point, the Leggistein, 1,192 yards in length, which is entered at 3,166 feet altitude and is left at 3,248 feet altitude. The church is now way below you as you round it for the third time.

Between Amsteg-Silenen and Göschenen, 24 kilometers, there are 21 tunnels including the three spirals. Göschenen is the northern entrance of the Gotthard Tunnel, third longest in the world. The run through it is made in 12 minutes. The tunnel is 15 kilometers, or 9.3 miles, in length.

The Gotthard Tunnel was bored in 1880, has excellent drainage, is very dry, double-tracked, of course, and is in marvelous shape.

After leaving the Gotthard, the line descends down through the four other spiral tunnels.

South of the Gotthard the first spiral tunnel is just south of Rodi-Fiesso and is entered at 2,999 feet and left at 2,881 feet. This tunnel is named the Freggio and is 1,715 yards in length. The line then drops down to the Prato Tunnel, 1,706 yards in length, which is entered at 2,812 feet and left at 2,730 feet. There are six other tunnels besides the two spirals in this group between Rodi-Fiesso and Lavorgo, 15 kilometers apart.

The next two spirals are in the beautiful Biaschina Gorge at Giornico and the first is named the Piano Tondo, 1,649 yards in length, and is entered at 1,824 feet altitude and left at 1,760 feet. Its twin adjoining it is the Travi Tunnel, 1,692 yards long, which is entered at 1,627 feet and left at 1,509 feet. This is really saving the climb. Joining these two spirals are two other tunnels.

The line then drops on down through beautiful scenery to Bellinzona, where the crews change. Leaving there there is another tough helper grade southbound from

Bellinzona to Rivera-Vironico, a distance of 14 kilometers and 6 more tunnels, then through the beautiful city of Lugano and its wonderful lakes, and on to the terminal at Chiasso, which is in Italy and immediately adjacent to the Italian Alps and Lake Como.

Just imagine what these grades must have been when they were working steam locomotives. They tell me 4 and 5 helpers were not unusual on both sides of the Gotthard. Of course, their power was small but then their tonnage was light and no grade was more than 2.7.

Due to the fact that the operation of the Gotthard is so interesting to so many people, I would like to give you this brief view into its interior so that you will realize what a wonderful operation it is and how it is controlled from Göschenen.

The double-line Gotthard Tunnel from Göschenen to Airolo has a length of 15 kilometers (9.3 miles), which formerly coincided with its train block section.

In 1938, this long block distance was reduced to half its length by an automatic block station and an axle counting device in the middle of the tunnel in order to facilitate maintenance and concurrent traffic operation.

In 1947, this block station was completed with 4 points as well as with all signals and electric interlocking installations as required for remote control from Göschenen.

These installations now give the possibility to take a fourth of the tunnel tracks out of operation, i.e., one half of the tunnel may have a double line and the other single line working, either on the left- or right-hand track.

The tunnel is now divided, in each direction, into three block sections, namely, block sections of 7 kilometers (4.4 miles) at both ends with another of 1 kilometer (signal station area) in the middle.

In the case of a normal double line working, all signals of the block station operate automatically.

During single line working either on the northern or the southern half of the tunnel, points and signals of the block station are operated from Göschenen.

The tracks of this block station called "Gotthard" are completely insulated and direct current is circuited at 12 volts. Any vehicle occupying these tracks is immediately detected.

The long tracks on both sides of "Gotthard," in the direction of Göschenen and Airolo, respectively, are equipped with axle counting.

The beginning and the end of these block sections are equipped with impulse magnets. Each axle passing one of these impulse transmitters gives one short current (impulse) which is recorded by an axle counter.

By this device, all axles of a train are counted when entering and leaving a section. If no carriage has been lost in the transit of that section, the counter shows "zero" and the corresponding signal will be cleared for the next train.

The earlier type of axle counters has given way to modern all-relay sets.

This axle counter system works from a minimum train speed of about 4 kilometers per hour (2.5 miles per hour) up to a maximum speed of 150 kilometers (93 miles).

The majority of European train lengths are counted by axles, not cars or wagons.

A cable with 50 wires reaching from Göschenen to the middle of the tunnel is used for the remote control of the signaling station "Gotthard."

The axle counters for the northern half of the tunnel are installed at Göschenen, those for the southern half at Airolo.

Interlocked signaling between Göschenen and Airolo is reciprocally dealt with by means of a special step switch transmitter, situated in Göschenen, for 12 different ways of line working between both points.

The signal lamps (40 volts, 20 watts) of the block signals are fed by traction current stepped down by transformers from 15,000 volts to 220 volts and further transformers. In case of failure of tension in the main line, batteries will supply the signals.

The block station "Gotthard" was put into service in 1947. It was soon observed that the block distance of about 6 kilometers (3.7 miles) between the stations on the northern valley line from Amsteg to Göschenen, ought also to be halved in order to solve the problem of increased traffic needs.

In 1950, the installation of three block stations was completed. The possibility of single line working with automatic block by means of axle counting was also realized on this line.

It must be remembered that the climate during winter is very rigorous and interruptions of the tracks by heavy snowfall or avalanche can happen.

Provision has been made to complete the automatic signaling equipment with automatic block stations also on the southern side of the tunnel during the next few years. Through these installations, the capacity of the Gotthard line will be doubled.

The signal and interlocking installations have been manufactured by "Integra" Wallisellen, Switzerland, the step switch transmission by "Albiswerke A. G.," Zurich, Switzerland.

Now that we have been over the Gotthard line and through the tunnel perhaps you would like to know something about the electric locomotives that were especially built for this service for hauling the passenger trains and some of the goods trains. This locomotive, Type AE 6-6, was especially designed for the service on the Gotthard line, which is characterized by very steep gradients (2.7 per cent. The locomotive is able to haul, in single-traction, trains up to a weight of 600 tons, that is, some 95 per cent of all Gotthard express trains. It is provided, therefore, to trail approximately the quintuple of its own weight while the trailing load of previously built types is limited to 0.6 to 3.6 times the locomotive weight. The speed on upgradients is 75 kilometers per hour (46.6 mph) as against 35 to 65 kilometers per hour (21.7 to 40.4 mph) in the case of locomotives hitherto existing.

Main data of the locomotive:

Length over buffers	18.4 m
Total wheel base	13.0 m
Diameter of wheels	1260 mm
Weight in running order	122 tons
Maximum starting tractive effort	33000 kg (72000 lb)
One-hour tractive effort at a speed of 74 km/h (46 mph)	21000 kg (46400 lb)
One-hour rating of the traction motors	6000 PS (5920 HP)
Maximum speed	125 km/h (77.8 mph)
Regenerative brake	

The mechanical part, built by the Swiss Locomotive and Machine Works at Winterthur, comprises the locomotive body and two 6-wheeled bogies. The body is a self-supporting unit in steel; the same principles of design were applied as in the case of the well-known Re4/4 locomotives and the lightweight coaches. The streamlined body leads to a modern and pleasant outward appearance of the locomotive and particularly to a small air resistance. The bogies were developed and built according to modern and efficient principles and methods of design and construction. They guarantee excellent riding properties and preserve the rails from heavy shocks and stresses in spite of the high axle loads. Each traction motor drives its corresponding pair of wheels through a flexible axle drive, type Brown Boveri, a design which was already successfully applied for the Re4/4 locomotive and other vehicles of the Swiss Federal Railways and other railway enterprises.

The following parts of the electrical equipment may be of special interest:

The high-speed air blast circuit breaker, installed in the roof; the radially laminated transformer and the high-voltage control, type Brown Boveri; the very robust traction motors; the electric brake equipment, type Oerlilon, which is able to brake the whole locomotive weight entirely electrically even on the steepest gradients; the perfected safety device; the automatic train control equipment and the electro-pneumatically controlled anti-wheel-slip brake.

In addition to the electric brake, the locomotive is equipped with a very efficient automatic air brake (R-brake), a special shunting brake which is controlled by means of compressed air, and a hand brake.

The driver's cabs, being arranged at both ends of the locomotive, are designed in such a way that the crew is able to work either standing or sitting. The large windows allow a very good view on the line. Further, the cabs are provided with carefully designed illumination, radiators and foot warmers, pneumatically controlled screen wipers, and an electric window heating.

64

The Simplon Tunnel

Ever since this author can remember the name Simplon has always been of the greatest interest to him, which I believe it is to all railroad engineers throughout the world and railroad men in general. Therefore it was a great pleasure to me to get a view of this tunnel, to ride the engines through it, and to have trains stop in the middle of it for me to see some of its workings in the interchange between the two bores in the center.

At a time when the construction of the Mont Cenis Tunnel had scarcely been put in hand, and when the plans for laying a line over the Brenner Pass were still being discussed and the Gotthard had entered the list with a Swiss Eastern Alpine Railway scheme, this Simplon had its plan for a direct tunnel. However, at the time of its realization the other schemes had long since been brought to fruition, for the Mont Cenis Line had already been open for 35 years, the Brenner almost 40 years, and the Gotthard 25 years. This was partly due to the fact that the Simplon Tunnel with its length of 20 kilometers presented greater difficulties than encountered in the case of any shorter tunnel. The main bore was pierced on February 24, 1905, at a distance of 9,385 meters from the southern portal. The total cost of the tunnel together with the parallel tunnel and the installations amounted to nearly 65 million francs. In 1912 the parallel tunnel was converted into a full-size tunnel and was put into service 10 years later, work unfortunately having been delayed by the First World War. Since that time the original electrical equipment has been converted for single-phase, alternating current of 15,000 volts at $16\frac{2}{3}$ cycles, and the extension to Domodossola has also been electrified so that now the heavy locomotives of the Swiss Federal Railways can run through from Vallorbe to Domodossola in each direction. The Simplon is essentially a funnel for traffic between northwest and southeast. This is evident from the nature of its express service for through international traffic. The two-class deluxe Simplon-Orient Express links up England and Paris with Milan, Venice, Trieste, Belgrade, Bucharest, Sofia, and Istanbul, and by its extensions, known as the Taurus Express, takes in Palestine, Serbia, Iraq, Iran, and Egypt. Moreover the Simplon has important connections with Genoa, Rome, and southern Italy as well as Brindisi for Athens, Egypt, and India. Since the opening of the Lötschberg in 1913, important connections for the north have been improved in the direction of the French Riviera exit at Brig.

Apart from the extensive traffic transit which is catered to by through express trains, the Simplon Line carries very substantial direct and internal traffic, the first having ever-increasing importance in winter. Connections with the main line are both numerous and important. At Vallorbe, the frontier station, Switzerland is entered and the railroad proceeds through the Jura Range toward Lausanne. (Geneva is reached by a branch line from Lausanne.) The line runs along the shores of beautiful Lake Geneva, through Montreaux where it connects with the

Montreux-Oberland with connections to Gstaad, thence to Interlaken. At Leuk you can see a steeply graded rock railway running to Leukerbad at the foot of the Gemmi Pass. At Visp there is a branch line to Zermatt. Brig is the junction for five lines: the main Simplon Line to Lausanne and Domodossola; the Bernese Alps Railroad, which climbs steeply up the northern side of the valley. The Lötschberg Railway leads through the Lötschberg Tunnel, the third longest in the world, 14,612 meters in length, to the Oberland, Bern, and the northern frontier. Coming from Paris through Bern you come down through the Lötschberg.

There are also connections for St. Moritz via the Oberalp and Furka Passes and for Zermatt at the foot of the Matterhorn. From Zermatt a very rugged rack railway ascends the Gornergrat, over 3,000 meters high. There are also two spiral tunnels on the approaches to the Lötschberg and it is a rugged fine railroad.

The Simplon is thus seen to be an important line. It is the shortest and quickest route between southeast and northwest Europe and serves the much frequented lake region of north Italy. There is much business on the Paris–Simplon–Milan Route, which takes a day without night travel with through coaches on the train for all three classes. Domodossola is the first station in Italy and the frontier gateway to that country.

The Lötschberg Railway, as already mentioned, is a route of 148 miles, operates through the Lötschberg Tunnel from Bern to Brig, and is the main connection. It has 30 fine electric locomotives, some 425 freight cars, and 140 passenger cars. Its heaviest grade is the usual 2.7 found on so many of the Swiss main lines and the maximum speed is 77 miles per hour. They have the regular 15,000 volt, 16⅔ cycles overhead wire conductor that the Swiss Federal Railway has and the engines are interchanged at times. I found this road in marvelous physical condition and all the tunnels were dry and well ventilated.

The loop and spiral tunnel at Dausse Mitholz provided some of the best engineering I have ever seen. The line runs the entire distance from Spiez all the way to Brig between a chain of mountains that are all named and are continuously from 2,000 to 4,000 meters in height. It is a beautiful ride.

The Rhetian Railway, of which there are so many fine pictures in this book, is the longest of the independently owned railways operating mostly in the canton (Swiss name for county) of Graubunden. This is the railroad that all the skiers, visitors, and tourists going to St. Moritz and Davos use. It is one of the most wonderful 3 foot 3 inch gauge roads in the world. It is completely electrified and 245 miles in length.

The Furka-Oberalp Railway is one of the most interesting I have ever ridden. It is a meter gauge road extending 60 miles which is all electrified, and there are 10 electric locomotives, some 40 multiple-unit cars, and 100 freight cars. In the rack sections they have grades from 11 to 17.9 per cent and in the adhesion sections, 4 per cent. They are permitted to make 18 miles an hour on the rack section and 34

66

miles an hour on the adhesive section. Their electrification is single phase of 10,400 volts of 16⅔ cycles overhead wire conductors. This railroad operates from Brig via Gletschen to Andermatt to Disents, where its connection has already been related with the Rhetian Railway. It also operates the line that I spoke of from Andermatt to Göschenen and going up and down that little hill and its tunnel on the 17.9 grade was of the greatest interest. You simply "explode" on Göschenen and the main Gotthard Line of the Swiss Federal Railways as you drop down. This is the heaviest railway grade the author has ridden with the exception of the Wengerlap and the Jungfrau Railroad, which will be discussed herewith.

The other light railway the author rode in Switzerland besides the last two mentioned was the Montreux–Oberland–Bernois Railway which also had meter gauge and was 45 miles in length, and it was a most interesting operation. Of the light railways he only missed the Gruyère and the 6-mile Gornergrat Road.

Riding the head end of the electrified Wengernalp Railway was most interesting. This is the longest of the complete rack railways and it operates from Leauterbrunne to Scheidegg, some 6 miles, and from Grindewald to Scheidegg, about 5 miles. There is 2 foot 7½ inch gauge and it is 12 miles in length. It has 15 electric engines and 41 passenger cars. They are now getting rid of all their electric locomotives. From Leauterbrunne with an altitude of 2,612 feet to Kleine Scheidegg at 6,762 feet, this railway had a 19 per cent grade and from Grindewald to Scheidegg 25 per cent which is like the Jungfrau Railway with which it connects. Scheidegg is the heaviest grade this author has ridden.

The Wengernalp Railroad has an uphill speed of 15 miles an hour and a downward speed of 9 miles per hour, very similar to the Jungfrau.

The Jungfrau Railroad—if you can imagine it—is practically all in a tunnel or a glacier, and an electrified tunnel at that. The electric current for it is supplied by foaming currents, the white and the black Lutchine. The current is conveyed by a copper wire overhead with high poles and is reduced from 7,000 to 650 volts to feed the trolley wire. On this railroad the speed limit up and downhill is 5.59 miles an hour. When this speed is exceeded in the slightest degree, an automatic brake is pushed down and the train is stopped. Precautions have also been taken in case of a sudden interruption of the current, the engines can when necessary be run downhill independently of the supply from the power station. The current necessary for braking is generated by the dead weight of the engine. The undercarriage of each engine supports both turning axles. Between these lie the two driving axles which are worked by two motors of 150 horsepower and 800 turns per minute each. The current is collected from the two-phase contact line by means of two contact valves. The rail current is collected from the undercarriage of the engine. The train consists of an engine and 3 cars which seat 40 passengers. Then they usually have a car for the skis on the rear end. The Wengernalp did also. The ski business is, of course, terrific. People come from all over

Europe to ski at these places. I also spent the night at Wengden, halfway up to Scheidegg on the Wengernalp Railroad, and that was another great ski spot.

The first station after leaving Scheidegg is Eiger Glacier Station, 1.24 miles distant with an altitude of 7,620 feet; then Eigerwand Station, 9,405 feet, 2.60 miles; Esmire Station, 2,370 feet, 3.53 miles; then the Jungfrau Station, 11,340 feet, 5.76 miles, which is the total length of the railroad, 5.76 miles equalling 9.3 kilometers. The maximum grades are 25 per cent on the cog section and 18 per cent on the adhesive section. Cast steel rails are used on iron ties, and the normal length of the rail is 34½ feet and the height of the rail, 3.93 inches. The cog rail is 11.48 feet in length and the weight of the cog rail is 74 pounds per meter or yard. The curves are up to 30 degrees and the gauge is 3 feet. The main tunnel begins at kilometer 2.2, 1.36 miles from Scheidegg, and ends at the Jungfrau Station. It is therefore 7.1 kilometers, or 4.40 miles, long and one of the longest tunnels there is. It is made of mountain limestone for 4 miles and then janeiss for the last 2. The road owns 11 locomotives, 7 of which are cogwheel engines, 4 for mixed operation, cogwheel and adhesion. Each locomotive has two 3-phase motors of 150 horsepower each. The average weight of each train is 30 tons. Twenty-one closed carriages, consisting of 12 carriages of 40 seats, totaling 480 seats, and 9 with 41 seats, totaling 369 seats. They own 4 open goods or freight cars and luggage vans and they also own a watertank car and one snowplow. The running time from Scheidegg to Esmeer is 42 minutes; Esmeer on to Jungfrau, 15 minutes more. The fares from Scheidegg to the Jungfrau are: single ordinary fare, 28 francs; return ticket, 40 francs. They give a big reduction for parties and schools. It seems to me that when you have seen this one your education is pretty complete, and when you are up there the hotel is right in the glacier and you look up at the Jungfrau 13,600 feet high and the other peak, the Monch, on the other side of it. It is a beautiful show and I saw a couple of Swiss Air Force jets doing their stuff among the peaks.

Yes, I cannot wait to return to Switzerland, and as I rode the engine out from Olten to Basle through the Hauenstein Tunnel, the engineer told me he had been with our Military Operating Battalions in Iran during the War, under Col. Frank Russell, and did I know him? It's a small world, I thought. Iran, California, the Southern Pacific, and here I am being asked by an engineer in Switzerland if I knew one of my best friends and a top S.P. railroader.

Passenger train on the Swiss Federal Railways leaving spiral tunnel on the northern approaches to the Gotthard Tunnel.

Double-headed passenger train coming out of the Wattinger Tunnel at Wassen on the Gotthard Line.

Goods train on the Swiss Federal Railways leaving the spiral tunnel near Wassen on the northern approaches of the Gotthard Line. The tonnage was light that day.

Passenger train on the Gotthard Line at Wassen. The village of Wassen, showing the church on the hill (upper left), which is rounded three times as you go through the northern spiral tunnels on the Gotthard Line.

Passenger train on the Gotthard Line at Wassen. The village of Wassen, showing the church on the hill (upper left), which is rounded three times as you go through the northern spiral tunnels on the Gotthard Line.

Goods train coming out of the Leggistein Tunnel on the northern approaches to the Gotthard Tunnel.

Passenger trains approaching Gotthard crossover in the middle of the Gotthard Tunnel, which is controlled from Göschenen. Note the fireman looking out on the "right side"—also the fine drainage, excellent ballast, and steel ties.

Type of lightweight fast train used between the big cities in the midlands of Switzerland. The locomotive is Class R 4-4.

The engineman is now on his
seat in the cab of the AE 6-6
Gotthard Line locomotive of
the Swiss Federal Railways.
The AE 6-6, described in the
text, is the latest locomotive
built for Swiss Federal Railways, and was specially designed for the Gotthard Line.

The AE 6-6 specially built for
the Gotthard Line.

The southern approaches to the Gotthard Tunnel showing aspects of the spiral tunnels in the Biaschina Gorge.

Southern approaches to the Gotthard showing entrance of the Travi Tunnel with the viaduct leaving from the Piano Tondo Tunnel above. The passenger train is in the middle. This is still the Biaschina Gorge.

Train is now on the upper line leaving the Piano-Tondo Tunnel, the second spiral tunnel in the Biaschina Gorge on the Swiss Federal Railways. Notice the excellent ballast, track and the steel ties.

Goods train entering the Travi Tunnel. Note how the automobile highways are always following the railroads. Anywhere you go throughout the world you will find this is so. There are few exceptions.

Funicular railway of the Rotim Power Station, which supplies power to the Gotthard Line, showing the cable car and the pressure pipes.

Type of snowshed or gallery, as they are called in Switzerland, for protection against snowslides and avalanches on the Gotthard Line. This is the typical Swiss Federal Railways snowshed.

Signal box or interlocking frame, as it is sometimes called, in the Zurich Station, Zurich, Switzerland. Note the shunting engine beneath the signal box.

The all-electric interlocking panels of the Zurich signal box interlocking frame. Note the uniforms the signalmen wear. The author spent some time in this box.

The great marshalling yard at Muttenz near Basle, probably the most important yard in all Europe.

The approaches to the Zurich Station.

The north portals of the Simplon Tunnel at Brig. In the center of the tunnel there is the Stazione della Galleria where it is possible to walk from one bore to the other.

The south portal of the Simplon Tunnel near Iselle. From Iselle to Domodossola, a distance of 19 kilometers, there are nine additional tunnels.

Passenger train running along Lake Geneva below the vineyards. Again we have the highway. This is the main Simplon Line.

The Gotthard Line near Sisikon along Lake Lucerne.

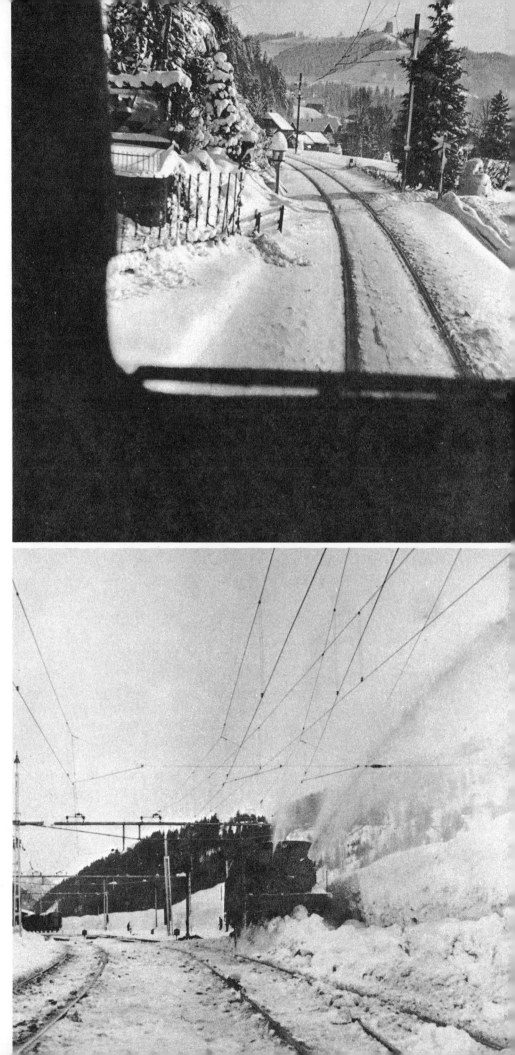

View from the cab of multiple unit train on one of the few Swiss Federal Railways narrow gauge lines, between Bern and Lucerne.

Type of snowplow used on the Swiss Federal Railways at work on the Gotthard Line.

The Swiss version of piggy-back, but not for the same reason as in the United States. These automobiles are being hauled on the railroad because of the snowbound Alpine passes—they were unable to get home. Therefore once again the railroad has to help. Here they have just come through the Gotthard Tunnel and are at Göschenen.

Engineer's side of the great AE 6-6 locomotive built especially for service on the Gotthard Line. Wheel on left is the automatic air brake. Lever is electric brake, the engine brake is not seen. The main throttle or controller is the wheel in the center. Note the series numbers beneath it. The reverse lever is to the right, the gauges, amperes, loads, etc., to the front; the panograph and other switches are underneath the speed recorders; oil gauges on the right with the headlight switches and other lights on the back right. Underneath, the light and timetable frame with which all Swiss motors are equipped. The timetable is there for the engine-man to see. Note the small grab iron for him to hold on to, as he stands up practically all the time. Directly below the controller wheel in the center is the deadman's brake panel, on which he must keep his foot.

Great engineering on the Albula line of the Rhetian Railway between Bergün and Preda, a horizontal distance of 3 miles surmounting a vertical rise of 1,368 feet and 35 degrees of curvature.

Train of the Rhetian Railway near Klosters with the aerial cable-
way Klosters-Gotschnagrat-Parsenn.

The Rhetian Railway near Monte Bello on the Bernina line with
the Bernina group of mountains in the background, the highest
and steepest adhesion railway in Europe. Its highest station is
Bernina Hospiz, 7,405 feet, and its gradient is 7 per cent.

Train of the Rhetian Railway on the Langwies Viaduct on the
Chur-Arosa line.

Fast train of the Rhetian Railway at the station of Scuol-Schuls-Tarasp, lower Engidan. This is the type of electric engine used in train service on this fine railway. The station is a typical one. Notice the big clock which is a standard feature of so many of the stations in Europe.

Through train of the Rhetian Railway between Davos, the gre ski center, and Klosters. Seven cars is the limit usually haule Note the fine track and ballast.

Train of the Rhetian Railway descending grade near St. Moritz.

Multiple-unit train of the Wengernalp Railway at Wengern Station. Note the rack in the middle of the track in the foreground.

Eiger Station of the Wengernalp Railway.

ilroading under the Jungfrau. Train of the Bernese-Oberland
ilroad hauled by electric motor.

Another view of the wonderful Jungfrau above the two lines of
the Wengernalp Railway near Wengern. Note the rack.

Train of the Wengernalp Railway on the 25 per cent grade approaching Scheidegg. The Wetterhorn, 12,000 feet high, is in the background. Notice the car for the skis on the rear end. People come from all over the world to ski here. There is a great influx from the British Empire. The English had a great deal to do with pioneering skiing in Switzerland and the ski business means a lot to these railroads in the winter.

Typical scene with the arrival of train in the large picture before this one at Kleire-Scheidegg at an altitude of 6,770 feet. This service is operated at frequent intervals during the winter months on the Wengernalp Railway.

Rotary snowplow of the Jungfrau at work. This is one of the seven cog wheel electric locomotives that are used in regular service.

This rotary snowplow is really clearing the line to the Jungfrau at Eiger Glacier on the Jungfrau Railroad at an altitude of 6,720 feet.

Line of the Jungfrau Railroad with Eiger Station in the background at 9,405 feet. The lovely Monch Mountain adjoins the Jungfrau in the background with an elevation of 12,300 feet.

France

IN the fall of 1944 the French no longer possessed a railroad system. Most of France's great rail centers had been pulverized by bombs. Twenty-six hundred bridges and 70 tunnels were destroyed. One hundred and fifteen main passenger stations and 24 key yards lay in ruins. Nothing remained but isolated and useless fragments of lines. Seventy-seven locomotive roundhouses—think of it!—19 repair shops, 700 towers, no longer existed. Eighty-two per cent of the locomotives, 80 per cent of the passenger cars, and 64 per cent of the freight cars were out of use. France was threatened with complete paralysis. The reconstruction of a railroad was the first job which faced her and the successful execution of this task was one of the major causes of her amazing recovery. For this, she gives due credit to the United States and also to the American railroaders who were in the country during the war. They did their best with what they had and before they left gave much cooperation and good ideas to the French. The 1,340 locomotives and 48,000 freight cars sent at the most critical moment by the United States and Canada were of inestimable aid.

The French railroads today are capable of coping with all the requirements of their new economy. They constantly look ahead, renew their techniques, equipment, and installations, and see to it that French technicians working in French factories forge the instruments that are absolutely indispensable if tomorrow's needs are to be met. The reconstruction of almost every signal bridge, including a great many built of reinforced concrete, the extension of automatic signaling to cover an additional 620 miles, 440 miles of electrification, 24 new yards of the most modern design, all these were proof of the revival. The many types of locomotives that have been on the French railways for years with their 2, 3, and 4 cylinders, compounds, various types of valve gear and hook-ups have now been reduced to only a few models. The same goes for the freight cars. The passenger cars are all lighter and sturdier, and the tare of the freight cars has been cut down and the loading capacity increased. Today France possesses the fastest trains in Europe. For my money, the railroad system is the finest of all French achievements.

The 1,300-odd 2-8-2 two-cylinder simple Mikados that were built by the Montreal Locomotive Works, the American Locomotive Co., and Baldwin Locomotive Works from 1943 to 1947 were the locomotives that really pulled France out of the hole. These engines have a tractive effort of 45,000 pounds with a 220-pound boiler pressure and 65-inch driving wheels. They have a tender capacity of 8,000 gallons, a fuel capacity of 12 tons, and the weight on the drivers is 253,800 pounds. These engines were used on passenger trains and were able to make the time on a good many of them; the author rode several during his stay in France. They are still in service and going strong.

The French had some fabulous steam power as compared with United States standards, all with small tenders. They had a 2-4-6-2 type, a four-cylinder compound, several big 2 8 0 four-cylinder compounds with 61-inch wheels, big 4-8-0's and other classes of compound Mikados. They had a 3-cylinder compound 4-8-4 with a tractive effort of only 40,000 pounds with 76-inch wheels. There were several classes of Pacific-type engines and all of them must have been horribly expensive to maintain and their performance was, I am sure, not too good.

Another locomotive they had was a 2-12-0 type. A great deal of money must have been spent on experimentation. It was therefore no small wonder that electrification was providing more comfort to their passengers and at greater speeds, and giving the railroad greater capacity, flexibility of operation, and savings in motive power maintenance. Since France lacks coal and does not produce any oil but does possess great electrical resources, there is great interest in electrification. The energy potential of the French dams has increased by half in the last ten years. Within a few years more, it will more than double. Twenty-seven hundred miles of railroad lines are electrified in France, representing one-tenth of the total mileage but one-third of the volume of rail traffic. The most important line electrified now is between Paris and Lyons, considered by the French to be the most important in Europe. Over it from one end to the other a total of 122 trains pass each day and this number rises to over 200 on certain days in summer. Electrification accounts for an annual saving under present conditions of 2,400,000 tons of quality coal vitally necessary to the French industries, and this figure will go to 2,750,000 tons after electrification projects are completed. The electrified portion of the French railway system uses 1,500-volt direct current. This system requires large-scale installations which are being built very naturally only on lines handling a heavy volume of traffic. The French engineers have developed a new system which makes direct use of 25,000-volt industrial alternating current, thus reducing installation costs. The low cost of installing this 25,000-volt electrification system is going to open up new horizons in the development of electrification in France.

The French track is remarkably good and their main lines ride very well. The gauge is 4 feet 8½ inches and the rail varies from 92 to 100 pounds. The ballast is usually broken stone or slag. They have very few bad curves and on the main lines not many hard grades. Their automatic signal system on the main lines is very good and they keep their tracks in good repair and watch them carefully. One hundred and twenty of their new interlocking towers are equipped with route levers controlling all other switches and signals from one station or section of the line. Their train dispatchers installed in all the principal rail centers can control and direct the movements of all trains on 8,700 miles of main line. These stations' functions also include the control of motive power and the distribution of freight cars, enabling French trains since the war to recover their former regularity and even to improve it. So they are today the leaders in punctuality among the world's railroads.

Since 1949, 96 per cent of French express trains and 99 per cent of suburban trains coming into Gare St. Lazare, the busiest station in the Paris region, arrived at the terminal on time.

The French have some centralized traffic control allowing them to run in both directions on both tracks of a difficult 17-mile section on the Paris-Lyons line.

French trains are the fastest in Europe. Every day they cover 12,500 miles at a speed exceeding 62 miles per hour and an additional 19,000 miles where the speed exceeds 56 miles per hour. They recently ran one of their new CC-type, 7,000-Class electric locomotives 150 miles an hour with a three-car train. The French say this locomotive also holds the world's speed record for distances exceeding 300 miles. Paris is connected with Normandy in 1½ hours, Brittany with Auvergne in 4 hours, Alsace in 5 hours, the French Alps in 7 hours, the Basque country in 9 hours, the Pyrenees in 10 hours, and the Riviera in 11 hours. That's pretty good going. Timetables have been planned in such a way as to allow passengers who spend a day in Paris to reach any city outside the capital in one evening or at most in one night. And across France from one tip to the other—from Lille to Biarritz, 653 miles; from Le Havre to Strasbourg, 700 miles; from Calais to Nice, 862 miles—no more than a day's trip is required. The running time on several of the faster trains carrying 900 passengers, about 600 tons, on daily trips from Paris to Dijon, 196 miles, is 2 hours and 32 minutes, an average speed of 77 miles an hour. Trains also run from Paris to Lyons, 318 miles, in 4 hours and 15 minutes at an average speed of 75 miles an hour.

The French railroad rates have all been revamped since the war and they are the lowest in Europe. Of course, in Europe many more people are on the railroads than there are in the United States.

In 1948, 645,000,000 passengers were carried, a number equal to the total carried by all the major United States lines combined. In Paris, St. Lazare Station alone sees 400,000 passengers pour daily through its gates. Of these, 60,000 pass between the hours of 6 and 7 P.M. at the rate of 1,000 a minute. Every summer between July 1 and August 31, 7,000,000 passengers leave Paris and return on main line trains. Today the French National Railways handle a volume of traffic which far exceeds that of prewar days, with much greater over-all efficiency. Steam locomotives have been reduced by 36 per cent and the daily running distance has been increased by 27 per cent. This railroad, whose name is Société Nationale des Chemins de Fer Français, has 5,700 stations and employs approximately 430,000 people. It is the largest business in France. Its Director, Louis Armand, deserves unstinted praise and credit for all that has happened. I have never met a more energetic or finer driving personality in any country that I visited.

He is a good railroader, knows his public relations, writes and delivers a fine speech, and is a fitting leader for the organization.

The Secretary, A. Dennis-Gravelle, is also one of the finest and most learned men I have met in the railroad business anywhere. He has a big job. The Secretary does a lot more work in France than he would do in the United States and is much more concerned with public relations and operations than anyone on the office staff would be in this country.

The French passenger cars are roomy and comfortable. Those which were built since the war were designed with an eye to the wishes expressed by the passengers in the course of a poll organized by the French National Railways in 1946. Like most European cars they are generally made up of several compartments of 6 or 8 seats. The compartments are isolated from each other and open into a corridor running along one side where passengers can move about and relax. The baggage goes in and out through the windows. How long people in the United States would put up with these compartments where passengers sit opposite each other and have no place for their feet, I would not venture to state in this book. They are great when they are empty but they are awfully full when they are loaded. However, parlor cars and cars of certain special trains have central corridors.

The railroad is divided into six regions for operational purposes.

Because of its unique geographic position, Paris is the hub of all the main European railway lines. International express trains connect Paris with all European capitals. Here one may take the Golden Arrow and the Ferry Train for Great Britain; the Bluebird and the North Star for Belgium and the Netherlands; the North Express for northern Germany and Denmark, Sweden, Norway, and Poland; the Orient Express for southern Germany, Czechoslovakia, Poland, and Austria; the Arlberg-Orient Express for Switzerland, Austria, Hungary, and Rumania; the Simplon Orient Express for northern Italy, Yugoslavia, Greece, Bulgaria, and Turkey; the P.R. (Paris-Rome) for Genoa, Rome, and Naples; the Barcelona Express and the Southern Express for Spain and Portugal. Besides these the great Blue Train connects Great Britain with the Riviera, crossing the whole of France via Paris. From Paris, trains take passengers to Brussels during lunch or dinner, to Amsterdam or Zurich in one evening, to London by train ferry, and to Hamburg or Milan in one night.

The French are very proud of their stations, particularly the many beautiful and famous ones in Paris, and it is a must for anyone interested in railroads to see them all.

All of the sleeping and dining cars on the above trains, as well as all the other sleeping cars on the many miles of railroads in Europe, are operated by the Compagnie Internationale des Wagons-Lits. Wagons-Lits corresponds to the Pullman Company in the United States. They operate first-class sleeping cars and their diners have extraordinarily big and palatable meals. There are, of course, sittings and there is no ordering. You are given whatever food they have. Whether the U.S. public would go for this arrangement I do not know. It is done now on a couple of very heavily patronized trains in the West where only one dining car is used, but I do not think people in the United States want such big meals, particularly at lunch, and they are also much more choosy in what they take. The Wagons-Lits sleepers have fine first-class compartments. The toilets are at the ends of the cars, but you can wash in your room. The baggage again goes through the windows. The sleepers are heated with coal stoves at one end of the car and have fine personnel in charge of them.

This author has the greatest respect for Wagons-Lits and one of the highlights of his railroad career was to meet their officials in Paris and to visit their directors' room, which is the finest I have ever seen. On the walls were maps of all the railroad companies Wagons-Lits does business with in Europe. Since each director represented a different country, the seats and pen-and-ink sets were all marked accordingly. It was a very interesting and wonderful room.

Yes, you have to hand it to the French railroads. They certainly made a comeback and are doing a fine job.

The great electric locomotive, of which the French are so proud, leaving Paris Norde with a fast passenger train. This locomotive is used for hauling express and mail trains, weighs 117 tons, is 65 feet long, and has 4,815 horsepower, which gives a gearing with a 990-ton train of 87 miles per hour. This locomotive works with direct current of 1,500 volts.

The signal box "tower" interlocking station at Montereau. With the help of a single switchman this box replaces 5 mechanical stations spread out over about 7 miles, allowing the working out of 350 different routes. Coming through Montereau on a locomotive or train will always be remembered, as the track is particularly good in this district and the curves are beautifully elevated.

Here is a typical French goods train hauled by electro-locomotive type DD. It has a total weight of 101 tons, a maximum speed of 65 miles an hour, and 3,240 horsepower. It is used in freight service and in handling some express and local passenger trains. It is rated for 65 miles an hour with 1,100 tons on level track. The picture was snapped at Montereau. Note the covered wagons at the head end of the train.

The fine French classification or marshalling yard at Villeneuve-St. Georges. This is the only yard I have seen outside the United States, Switzerland, Chile and Japan, which is equipped with retarders. Here is a car going down through one of them. Note the modern and snappy retarder control tower on the left. This yard is capable of handling 4,000 cars a day.

A locomotive with which the French broke the world's speed record. On February 21, 1954, the CC 7121, with these three cars weighing 122 tons, reached a speed of approximately 150 miles an hour between Dijon and Beaune. They are fine locomotives and the author has ridden many miles on them.

The diesel locomotive in France, type 040DE. Here it is used for the hauling of freight trains along side tracks and switching of trains in stations with two different working systems: (1) their railway line system which runs under the most economical conditions for the use of diesel power; (2) the belt, terminal breffer, dead-end system which uses the diesel's efforts which are very gradual. They have been carefully studied in France with a view to reducing the upkeep to a minimum weight in operation. This one weighs 74 tons, has an over-all length of 48 feet 5 inches and a maximum speed of 50 miles per hour. They like them, of course, for switching and for spots where there is no electrification.

The new automotive self-propelling fast trains of the SNCF are made up of double elements, as they say. An automotive self-propelling locomotive they call a "tender," while we in the U.S. call it a "trailer." The first automotives have been equipped with two diesel motors of 300 horsepower each. The next 20 will be put in service in 1955 and will have a single 750 horsepower diesel motor. All these automotive trains which supposedly will reach a speed of 88 miles an hour are destined for long-distance runs along nonelectrified tracks such as from Lyon to Bordeaux, Strasbourg to Lyon, Paris to St. Etienne, Genève-Port-Bou, and even for international trains such as Basle-Brussels and Paris-Amsterdam. Director Armand is right up-to-date with his diesels where he cannot get electrification.

Interlocking system with ball bearings at dispatch center of Acheres. This control table includes as many vertical tubes as there are tracks in the group of sidings. When a railroad car runs past a butt terminal buffer, the butt switchman pushes the button corresponding to its track, dropping down the tube in the disconnecting center a ball which follows the progress of the railway car and controls the switches. This is one we do not have in the United States.

Multiple-unit train in the United States and automotive self-propelling element in France. This one is in the southeast suburbs of Paris. They are excellent trains, both in car and on the head end. I rode several of them. Each car is made of unoxidizable steel, 18 per cent chrome, and 8 per cent nickel. The train accommodates 265 passengers. It has 154 seats. Its four 330 horsepower motors allow it to reach a speed of 75 miles an hour in 1 minute and 20 seconds.

The French, like the Swiss, have many types and classes of electric locomotives. Here is the 2D-2 9101 which weighs 158 tons and has a nonstop run power under 1,350 volts of 4,400 horsepower, and a one-hour run power of 4,880 horsepower. It is geared for 87 miles an hour. In March, 1954, one of this class of locomotives was operated a distance of 32,078 miles, which is said to be, and I believe it to be true, the world's distance record for miles per month made by any locomotive anywhere.

This picture shows one of them hauling a passenger train near Fontainebleau. Notice the typical French country and the fine 4-track railroad with the excellent ballast and elevated curves.

Here is a good look at a European freight car close up. Note the 4-wheel trucks, the bumpers, the bumper-type coupler. This car is equipped with air brakes. Many of them, particularly in the British Empire, have nothing but hand brakes. Here you can see how a retarder works a braking effort on the wheels as the car comes through at the Jurisy marshalling yard at Villeneuve-St. Georges.

The main dispatch center of traffic at Dijon. From this center are controlled all the switches and signals along the double-track section Blasy-Bas-Dijon, 15 miles, which controls reverse running on both tracks for that distance, which, of course, at busy hours allows them a much greater density along a line which has particularly heavy traffic.

This is the French version of CTC. Notice the typical European dispatcher's sheet in front of the dispatcher. The sheet already contains the lines, each representing a train; times and stations are already down. If an extra train is run, the dispatcher draws a new line. If the train gets off its schedule, he makes a notation with another line.

The author was greatly honored while in Paris to be made an honorary member of the Club Intercontinental des Transports, the great traffic club of France. They were also kind enough to send his 1954 card to him in the United States.

Pass on the French National Railways, Société Nationale des Chemins de Fer Français, presented to the author while in the country.

Beautiful bronze medal that Director Louis Armand, General Manager of the French National Railways, had struck off when the electrification was opened between Paris and Lyon in June of 1952. Note their prize electric engine on the medal.

Back of the medal given in celebration of the opening of the Paris-Lyon electrification.

ELECTRIFICATION DE PARIS A LYON

JUIN 1952

HIER LIBRE ET IMPETUEUX, AUJOURD'HUI DOMPTE, MAIS NON OPPRIME, LE RHONE CONCOURT AVEC FIERTE AU TRIOMPHE DU RAIL ET DU PROGRES HUMAIN

SNCF

ED. HERRIOT

Belgium

NOWHERE that I railroaded was I more surprised and impressed than I was with the Belgium National Railway Company, known as the Société Nationale des Chemins de Fer Belges. It is beautifully operated by men who know their business and has some very excellent motive power and fine electrification. It will probably be getting more diesels in the near future and now has many diesel railcars.

I was told that Belgium has more railroad track per square mile than any other country in the world. The railroad is electrified from Antwerp to Brussels and from Brussels to Charleroi. The gauge is standard—4 feet 8½ inches—and there are 3,100 miles of railroad with 3,051 locomotives and some 90,000 freight cars.

The road made startling and wonderful comebacks after World War II and a great deal of new building was carried out. Since the war, the Belgians speak very highly of our American railroaders. Belgium's signaling is excellent and they have a unique system employing a stationary signal to call attention to the home signal.

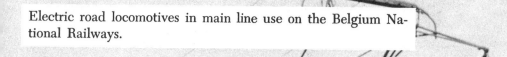

Three of these locomotives were built. They have 86-inch driving wheels. The author personally rode this one. The majority of them run main-line service from Brussels to the Dutch frontier on the Brussels-Amsterdam trains.

Excellent high-wheel Pacific-type locomotive in use on the Belgium National Railways. These locomotives are all over the steam part of the system and are hauling fast passenger trains from Luxembourg to Brussels.

Note the roller bearings on the tender and the type of big coke coal—practically briquettes.

The Belgians have wonderful multiple-unit cars of various classifications—they are most comfortable and can handle many people in suburban service. Cars like these are used between Brussels and Charferol and are some of the finest the author has ever ridden, both from the head end and back in the cars.

Italy

THE Italian State Railways took a hard beating during World War II and suffered considerable damage and loss of equipment. They lost some 25 per cent of their track and 67 per cent of their electric locomotives, which was a terrible blow to them. Next to France, Germany, Belgium and Japan, I believe they have put their railroads back in better shape than other countries that were badly damaged.

The Italian State Railways operates almost all of the railroads in the country for a total route length of more than 10,000 miles. The electrified portion between all the chief cities is 3,480 miles long. They have 1,562 electric locomotives. The author rode five different classes of electric road locomotives while in the country. The gauge is standard—4 feet 8½ inches—and there are few grades over 3 per cent. In Sicily there are grades over 7 per cent.

The country is full of railroad tunnels—it must have been exceedingly easy for the belligerents to tie up the railroads. The 1,850 tunnels have a total length of 574 miles. The longest is between Bologna and Florence and is 11½ miles long. It is named the Apennine and is the world's second longest tunnel.

The Italian signaling is good. They operate some very good trains and the track is much better than you might expect. They are good railroaders and the operating heads and officials of the road know their business and are first-class in every respect.

One of the most interesting and beautiful rides I have ever had on a locomotive or on any railroad was between Terreno, Italy, and Modane, where the French National Railways takes over. I was riding the electric motor of the crack RP (which means Rome–Paris) on a solid *wagon-lit* (Pullman sleeper) train, and the trip upward that night through all the villages with a full moon and a fresh fall of snow was something to be remembered, as was the famous old Mont Cenis tunnel, nearly 8½ miles long. Then at Modane I rode another electric engine down to Chambery-Challes-les-Eaux, which was just as beautiful. This was the Italian and French part of the Alps.

The new Rapido from Milan to Naples by day. A multiple-unit train with many new features, of which the Italians are rightfully very proud. It is pictured here in the wonderful new terminal in Rome, which is one of the most palatial the author has ever seen.

Note that the engine crew is in the dome of the leading car and that the lower level is reserved for the passengers who observe operations from the head end.

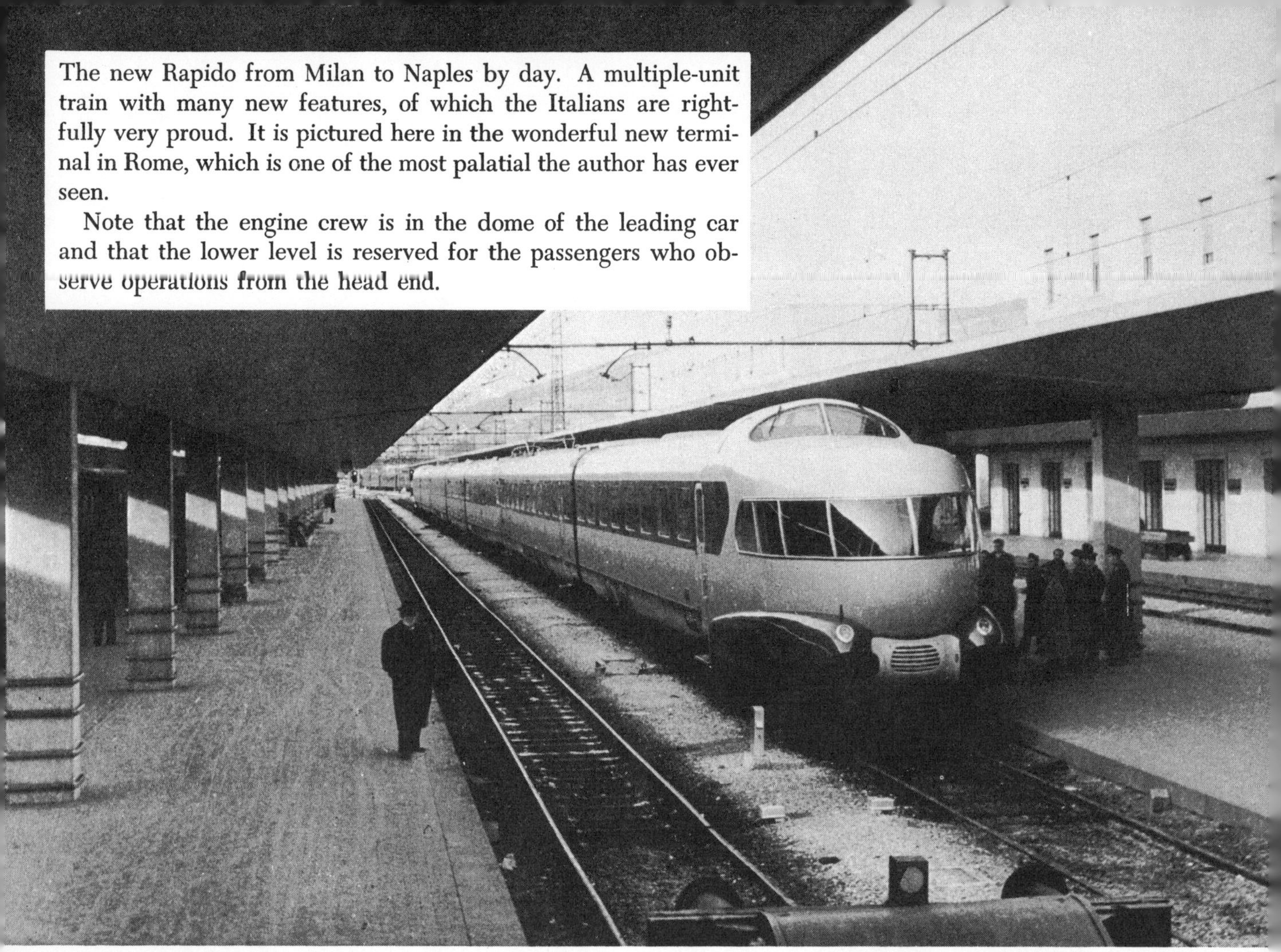

The Rapido boasts a newsstand. Notice the Paris edition of New York *Herald Tribune* on the stand. This is one innovat that has not been tried out by the railroad idealists in the Uni States.

The electric train communication service, loud speakers and radio on the Italian State Railways Rapido.

Interior of the Rapido's restaurant car. All the crack diners on the European lines are operated by Wagons-Lits and you are served tremendous meals at from two to four sittings. You are given tickets telling when to eat. The author does not believe this type of service would ever be popular in the United States even though the trains are highly crowded. But it is being used on a couple of crack trains in the United States.

Spain

THE Spanish are great people and they are good railroaders, not only in the mother country but in other countries where Spanish is spoken. The National Railway network of Spain today is composed of four railroads, the government having taken them over in 1941. (There are also some other companies operating narrow-gauge railroads, mostly meter gauge, totaling about 2,800 miles. These companies are not nationalized but they are subject to government control of operations.) The gauge is 5 feet 6 inches and they operate about 8,000 miles of track. Of this total some 325 miles are electrified. There are 3,200 locomotives in the country using steam, 95 electric, 85 oil, 3,200 passenger cars, with 75,000 freight wagons. They now have over 100 miles of track with automatic signals; most of the dispatching is manual-blocked from station to station. They have some big 2-10-2 freight engines, operate some Garretts, and have fine 4-8-2 passenger and fast freight locomotives with a tractive effort of 48,000 pounds with 227-pound boiler pressure and 68-inch wheels. Their Santa Fe types have 58,000 pounds tractive effort for the same boiler pressure and 61-inch wheels. Their tenders are small, carrying only 6,100 gallons of water and 7 tons of coal.

They have many named trains, of which the Andalusia Express between Madrid and Seville is one of the most famous, and they operate quite a few fast freight trains, many of them hauling fruit, fish, and other perishables.

The longest tunnel in Spain is 4,423 yards of single track. Most of the rail is 91 pounds. Their curvature is no worse than 6 degrees and their grades are up to 2 per cent in the flat areas and up to 4 per cent in the mountains. The Talgo train is, of course, their big talking point today and they are very proud of it.

The Talgo train, built in the United States by the American Car and Foundry Co., started its regular passenger service on the Madrid-Hendaye line of the Spanish National Network in July of 1950, and has covered over a million kilometers with not too many serious mechanical difficulties.

Two Talgo locomotives at the entrance of the special maintenance shops at Madrid.

de up in sections with a seating capacity of 160, the Talgo
es 8 hours and 40 minutes to go from Madrid to Irun, which
resents a saving in time of about 25 per cent over the conven-
al trains.

Looking through the articulated sections of the train, notice the effect of continuity in this picture.

Germany

DUE to the fact that Germany is now divided into Eastern and Western Zones, the German State Railway operates in East Germany with a total of 8,000 miles and 155 miles of electrification, while the German Federal Railways, which is larger by far, operates 21,700 miles in the Western Zone with 143 miles of narrow gauge. In all they operate about 50,000 miles of track, including 1,038 miles of electrification. Both of these roads have a 4 foot 8½ inch standard gauge.

As most of my time has been spent on the lines of the Federal Railways, this portion of the book will be more or less concentrated on them. The Germans made a remarkable recovery from the shellacking they took in World War II. Cities like Hamburg, Bremen, Hanover, and Dusseldorf have really come back. I was amazed by the way the railroad yards have been rehabilitated and the way the motive power has been put back in shape. The track is remarkably good, some of the best in Europe, and it appears to me that the Germans are excellent railroaders, both in the shops, the towers, and in train service.

The Scandinavian Express was one of the best trains I have been on in Europe.

Like some of the other roads, the Germans put one conductor on the train as operating conductor and another one as clerical conductor. A third man rides in the mail van on the rear, in charge of the international mail when it is carried. Most of their mail vans have a small cupola in the top; in fact, the Germans try to make up all their trains with a cupola car on the rear end so the guard can sit up and look the train over.

The Germans have several classes of lightweight and high-wheel 4-6-2 Pacific-type engines which do the majority of their passenger work. Their tractive efforts run between 31,000 and 35,000 pounds with 220-pound boiler pressure and 78-inch driving wheels. They also have a 4-6-4 engine with a tractive effort of only 32,100 pounds. But then, of course, some of these roads do not need big starting effort on account of the light weight of the trains. When you get a passenger train of 450 or 500 tons you have a big train. For freight service the largest German engine and one of the largest I have seen in Europe was their Class 45 2-10-2 type with a tractive effort of 67,000 pounds, with the same boiler pressure of 280 pounds which so many of their locomotives have, and 63-inch driving wheels. They also have some 3-cylinder 2-10-0's but this 45 Class is pretty good for drag freight, though of course they are handicapped by their small tanks and their fuel capacity. The German Federal Railways naturally burn coal and they continually wet it down more than any other road I have been on. Their engine crews have the timetables in racks on each side of the cab and are most efficient when it comes to small details. This road has more than 12,000 locomotives which burn coal for fuel, some 450 electric and over 600 diesels, some 28,000 passenger cars, and approximately 60,000 freight cars. They have no grades to speak of. They now have rail as heavy as 100 pounds in weight.

Of course, a great many Germans do not have automobiles, and there is a large movement of bicycles in the baggage cars because of the great amount of bicycling all over the country, particularly during the summer months.

The engineering work that impressed me most in Germany was the bridge and its approaches over the Kiel Canal, near Lübeck. This was beautiful engineering with a 1.5 per cent grade and big horseshoe fills on either side. The engine was slipping all the way up but we made it.

S. Kip Farrington Jr.'s pass on the Deutsche Bundesbahn (German Federal Railways).

Sweden

THE Swedish State Railways operate about 10,500 miles—about 17,000 kilometers in Sweden. (There are only about 200 miles of narrow gauge lines that are privately owned today.) This mileage is standard gauge, 4 feet 8½ inches, with some 315 miles of meter gauge and 1,140 miles of 2 foot 11 inch gauge. Of this standard gauge total 3,421 miles are electrified, and the railroad boasts 676 engines as against 855 for steam operations, a great many of which are now being retired.

The Swedish State Railways are very far-reaching, for Sweden is a far-stretching country. From Trälleborg in the south to Rigsgransen 200 kilometers north of the Arctic Circle, the traffic is run through all kinds of weather the year around.

The author has had the honor and privilege to look this railroad over at first hand from the head end and the rear end, from an electric dynamometer car, and from "personal carriages," which business cars are called on many European roads.

In Elsinore Sound, between Elsinore, Denmark, just north of Copenhagen, and Hälsingborg, Sweden, on the other side, it is possible to take the big tuna and see the railroad operations in two countries at the same time. Denmark is a great little country and its railroads have a very excellent switching movement. The car ferries go back and forth between Elsinore and Hälsingborg as they do between Copenhagen and Malmö. The ferries carry the cars for the crack Scandinavian Express. The ore-move is from Narvik, above the Arctic Circle, down to Boden and the port of Lulea on the Baltic Sea, and it is a very fine one. The railroad takes up to 3,500 tons in this movement, which is the heaviest weight that I know of in all of Europe. In Sweden they have grades up to 2 per cent and this tonnage is handled with only one helper. There is also a good ore-move from Trondheim.

The Swedes are fine railroaders. It was a pleasure to be with them and I learned much. T. H. Thalander is one of the best operating men I have ever known and is a genius in electricity. He served as Chief of Electrification for the Swedish State Railways for some years, as Vice President of Operation, and now has a position with the Swedish government. He has written amazing books in English, one on the American railroads and several on his own road, of which he was prouder than any other man I have ever met. He was, of course, very electrical-minded. The electrification of the Swedish State Railways has meant a great deal in transport economics to them, has helped their system of communications, and given

127

them a valuable independence which has improved the balance of trade, lowered their transport cost, and strengthened the economic position of the State Railways. Since Sweden has no oil wells but ample water power and adequate coal deposits, it was the natural thing for them to do.

The Swedish State Railways have many fine new freight cars and haul excellent tonnage for Europe, on the average of about 1,100 tons in their electrified freight service. They have four different types of electric locomotives.

The fast multiple-unit service between Stockholm and Gothenburg is nonstop, and these trains run at frequent intervals throughout the day.

The Swedish State Railways boast of the only electric dynamometer car, I believe, in the world. This was designed by Mr. Thalander himself and also serves as a business car as well. The car contains three double staterooms, one darkroom for developing photographs, a kitchen, a toilet with two basins and a bunk, and another room for the cook. Out of the dynamometer end of this car, you are able to get the number of poles, the stations at ten-second-interval time, low voltage on the contact line with pantograph if no contact, acceleration of the vertical movements of the pantograph, the train speed, the height of the pantograph power shoe over the rail, and the wind velocity. There is a switchboard of instruments— instruments which tell the oil temperature of the transformers in the car, pressure in the compressors, insulation in the car, the miles per hour, the wind velocity, the power consumed by the locomotive, recording power meter, recording ampere meter, and the recording energy meter. At the lounge end there are six chairs in the parlor, as they call it, plus a table, and meals are served there. This car has a dome, but what was most interesting was that you go up and down in the dome in an elevator seat which holds three people, and you sit in this chair as you watch the action of the pantograph on the wire, which was the reason for the dome. You press a button to go up and down.

swedish State Railways dynamometer business car. Notice the
KF roller bearing installation. While this roller bearing bears
he author's initials and he is kidded about it in many places, he
s a Timken man and believes they are the finest bearings made
oday. This belief did not, of course, go over very well in Sweden.

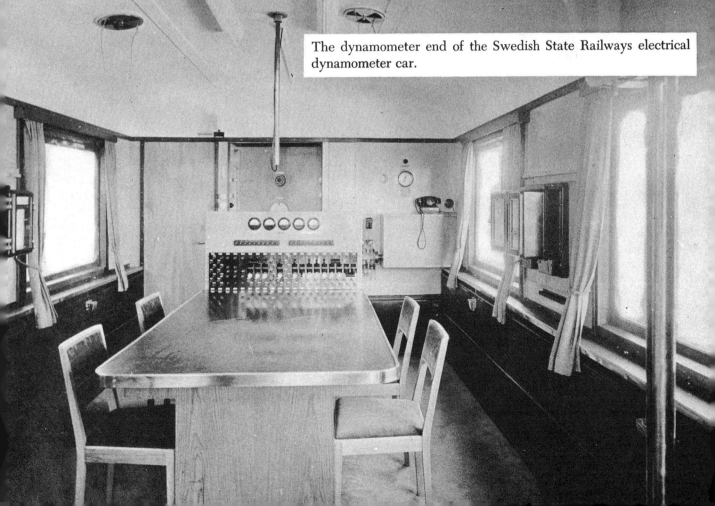

The dynamometer end of the Swedish State Railways electrical
dynamometer car.

Other end of the dynamometer room in the rear of Swedish State Railways dynamometer car, with chair in the dome holding no occupants.

T. H. Thalander, Sweden's great railroader and electrification expert, sits between Mr. and Mrs. Farrington in the dynamometer car's elevator chair rising to the dome above.

Bedroom on Swedish State Railways dynamometer car made up for day use, with gauges on the wall.

The parlor and dining end of the dynamometer business car.

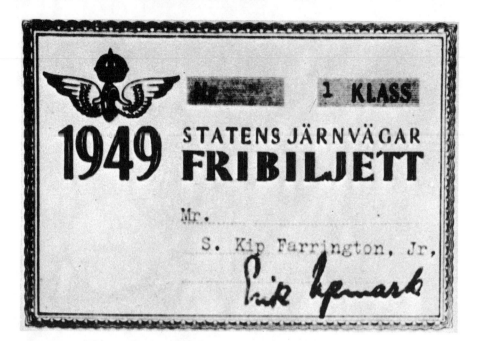

The author's pass on the Swedish State Railways.

The Swedish State Railways multiple-unit light express train carrying 178 passengers, the Göteborgaren mile-a-minute train between Göteborg and Stockholm. Notice the fancy costumes on the Swedish engine crew. Mrs. Farrington was presented with an entire station-master's outfit, brass buttons, insignia, flags, and all.

Etiquette and protocol among the railroaders in Sweden and Norway is as good as it is in Germany and Switzerland.

Norway

I HAD looked forward to making an inspection of Norway and her railways, but I never realized the beauty and ruggedness of the country and the amount of snow that fell at such a low altitude. It is, of course, the latitude of the country that brings the snow; you are over the timber line at about 3,500 feet. Norway certainly ranks at the top for heavy falls of snow and the continued effort on the part of the railroad to combat it. As I have always been interested in the difficulties of winter operation in big snowfall territories, I was immensely pleased to get a look at what the fine railroaders of the Norwegian State Railway have to go through.

It was my privilege to ride this road from Charlottenberg to Oslo coming in from Sweden, from Oslo to Trondheim, from Oslo to Kristiansund, and over the wonderful main line from Oslo to Bergen on which I spent some time. Besides that, I was up at Narvik looking over the ore-move at the junction with the Swedish road. A short stretch of track leads to the Swedish frontier way up in the north.

Electrification is rapidly taking place in Norway, and rightfully so, as they have great hydroelectric potential. Electrified routes now extend for more than 700 miles with 900 miles of track and a single-phase system of 15,000 volts with the overhead catenary as conductor. The total length of the railroad is about 2,720 miles in routes, 3,400 miles of line. The gauge is standard, 4 feet 8½ inches, and the rail goes up to 101 pounds on the main line in particular. Their ballast is crushed rock and they are gradually replacing their gravel ballast. They also have a stunt of laying peat under the tracks in all new construction in order to prevent damage due to freezing and the heavy thaws they encounter. Their curves are not bad— not many more than 10 degrees on the main line but the branches have them up to 16 degrees.

The heaviest grades between Oslo and Bergen, the most used portion of the railroad, are not more than 3 per cent and their sharpest curve on this line is only 9 degrees or a trifle over. Sixty-two miles per hour is the highest speed permitted. The road boasts 719 tunnels for a length of 115 miles, mostly rock boring, and the line from Oslo to Bergen alone has 100 snowsheds and 99 tunnels. They have good clearances and have over 3,000 bridges. The country took an awful beating in the war and 105 bridges were destroyed, many of which have been permanently rebuilt; in fact, the great majority. The Norwegians are very fine railroaders and I was amazed how fast they could make repairs and take care of breakdowns.

Their passenger trains are good, their crews fine. I had a pilot named Sande taking me around who was one of the best railroaders I have ever met. His position corresponded roughly to that of an assistant superintendent in the United States. Unlike some of the European roads, the Norwegian State Railway has business cars. All in all I was very much impressed with their operations. They are doing the best they can with what they have. They have not built a steam engine in some thirty years and with electrification coming on probably will not get many more. They have some diesels in service between Oslo and Trondheim and probably will buy a few more. They are courageous and forward looking.

On the 309 miles from Oslo to Bergen there are 70 kilometers of snow fences and 60 kilometers of wooden tunnels which help comprise the 99 tunnels, plus the 100 snowsheds which are separate. The rail here is all laid in 15-foot lengths. It was on this railroad, at Finse, that the 1952 Winter Olympics were held. Just west of Finse in the heart of the snow country is Myrdal, the junction point for the electrified railroad going down to a place called Flam on a fjord. This line, I should guess, would not give them more than 20 passengers a day in the summer, and I should say that if they got two carloads of freight out of there in a week it would be a great deal. In the winter I doubt very much if they get anything. This branch runs 12 miles from Myrdal to Flam, though the air distance is only 9 miles. The steepest grade is 4.8 and the difference in altitude is 2,835 feet on the 12-mile stretch. The line was built on embankments and through 20 tunnels—they crossed under 3 rivers with tunnels instead of bridges. The terrain was so difficult that it cost 26 million kroner, or an average cost of 13,000 kroner per meter, or 24 pounds per foot. I have just told you what they are getting out of there right in the middle of nowhere. I cannot think of any other electrified branch line that I have ever seen compare with it. Can you imagine spending all that money for such an undertaking with that small amount of traffic?

When you get near Bergen you are in the midst of the famous salmon fishing rivers and the railroad runs right alongside many of them. You won't find better snow fighters anywhere than the Norwegians and they have many excellent methods of combating it. I believe all United States railroaders might learn something about snow fighting if they went over there and had a look. The Norwegians have rotary plows and also pilot plows to haul in back of the rotaries. They have spreaders and a plow for use between the rails that I have not seen in any other country. They are truly wonderful people and wonderful railroaders. Perhaps I am partial to them because all of the hooks we use to catch the big fish on are made by the Mustad people in Oslo.

Train #602, crack daylight train from Bergen to Oslo, arriving at Myrdal on a winter morning.

Great picture of a rotary snowplow clearing the main Bergen-Oslo line at Finse where the 1952 Winter Olympics were held.

The Flamdal Canyon at Myrdal showing the snowsheds on the left, with the main line on top, and the branch line going down to Flam below. The river and the automobile road are coming down on the right. The highways get everywhere. Notice all the switchbacks on this road.

Type of snowscraper hauled behind a locomotive working at kilometer 250 near Al on the Norwegian State Railway.

View from a rotary snowplow being pushed out of a snowshed near Myrdal. That's a pretty formidable looking drift ahead.

Diesel-electric three car set in service on the Norwegian State Railway. They comprise the equipment of the Bergen and Doore expresses.

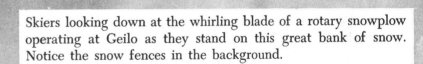

Norwegian State Railway train #602 standing at Finse several hours late in the middle of a snowstorm. Note the pilot plow.

Skiers looking down at the whirling blade of a rotary snowplow operating at Geilo as they stand on this great bank of snow. Notice the snow fences in the background.

Norwegian State Railway coal train at Malmtog with electric freight motor. These engines will haul up to 1,000 tons.

Another type of Norwegian plow and doser, working at Ustaose on the Norwegian State Railway.

Rotary snowplow working at Ustaoset on the Norwegian State Railway.

The Norwegians call this a "spornser" and haul it behind a caboose, locomotive or plow. It is the first time I have ever seen a pilot plow hauled behind a train but here is the evidence.

All of the Norwegian State Railway's snowsheds are in excellent condition and heavily and sturdily built with excellent clearances.

Norwegian railway conductor with his brass buttons and cap and trim. The red band means train service, blue band would mean engine service, a yellow band would mean clerical service. Note the large and heavy punch in the conductor's left hand and his starting flag which he waves after he gets the bell, whistle, or flag signal from the stationmaster, who has the responsibility of starting the majority of the trains.

The motorman's compartment of the Norwegian State Railway's electric three-car set. (In the picture above, the conductor is standing in front of the cab.) Note the timetable stand with the light over it to hold the timetable, which is always kept in view on so many of the world's railroads. Some of the old-time engineers in the United States should see the valve that is rigged on the Norwegian coal-burning locomotives, so that the engineman opens and shuts the fire door with his left hand with every scoopful the fireman shovels in.

General type of rotary snowplow in use on the Norwegian State Railway with coal tender. These are usually pushed by one locomotive, headed in the opposite direction, sometimes, of course, by two or three.

Here is the locomotive that does it all—the general all-purpose 4-8-0 type built in the early 1920's is the workhorse in the Bergen District on both freight and passenger service. In all these snow pictures that you have seen all the snowplows were handled by this locomotive, built some thirty years ago. It has some 31,000 pounds tractive effort, 63-inch wheels, Walschaert's valve gear, and a boiler pressure of 200 pounds. This line is now electrified from Bergen to Voss and it won't be long before it is completely electrified. This little locomotive has done a remarkable job. The only other larger steam power in Norway is one 2-8-4 type locomotive built in Germany.

Great Britain

THE British Railways are now divided into six regions: Scottish, Eastern, Southern, Western, London Midland, and Northeastern. They are all operated by the government. British railways have excellent signaling and it is a good thing they do because their density of traffic is very high. They have excellent dispatching from tower to tower on two or more track operations. There is much fast running which is all left-hand with left-hand operation. North Americans would be interested to know that there are no bells on the locomotives, no headlights as we know them, no marker lights, no air signal lines, no air conditioning, no brakes at all except hand brakes on the freight or goods trains, no air brakes on the passenger trains, vacuum brakes being used. Their tenders are small, they scoop water at certain places and their average 90-pound rail is built on chairs. There is no grade in the British Isles worse than 2.78 and that only for a distance of two miles. All of their grades better than 2 per cent are under ten miles in length. A 400-ton freight train would be a very big one in England, and their passenger trains probably do not average 250 tons. They have no roller bearings, no automatic couplers; in fact, there are no automatic couplers in all of Europe. Many of their bridges are very interesting and are excellently built.

I have ridden their dynamometer cars, visited their locomotive testing plant at Rugby, and have also ridden all their Pacific-type engines with their various valve gears, injectors, reverse levers and throttles (called regulators in England). Their 10-wheel-type locomotive is still the workhorse on their 19,000 miles of railroad.

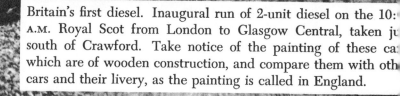

Britain's first diesel. Inaugural run of 2-unit diesel on the 10:
A.M. Royal Scot from London to Glasgow Central, taken ju
south of Crawford. Take notice of the painting of these ca:
which are of wooden construction, and compare them with oth
cars and their livery, as the painting is called in England.

The Toby Express hauled by one of the English workhorses,
4-6-0 type locomotive. Note the excellent ballast and the ra
on chairs.

7:40 A.M. Penzance to Wolverhampton Express at Dainton Summit signal box, South Devon, with locomotive 1019.

Locomotive 1010, the County of Caernarvon, another of the famous County class workhorse British locomotives, with the 5:30 A.M. London-Penzance Express at Stonycombe Quarry. The number 120 signifies the locomotive terminal, or shed, as it is called in England, to which this locomotive belongs.

The Atlantic Coast Express leaving Waterloo (London), as they say in England, hauled by the Merchant Navy Class locomotive 35016, 4-6-2 type, named the Elders Fyffes. All of this class named after ships and steamship companies.

Scottish region which I always remember for its grouse moors, golf courses, and vistas, not to mention the heather and the railroads. Here we have the 9:30 A.M. Glasgow (Queen Street) to Edinburgh via the West Highland Line and Crianlarich, where the picture was snapped.

Notice the signal box and the signals for left-hand running.

The engine is 61344, a 4-6-0 type from the Eastfield Depot.

Mexico

THE Ferrocarril del Pacifico operates from Nogales on the United States border of Arizona all the way down to Guadalajara, where it connects with the National Railway. This was formerly the Southern Pacific of Mexico. It is standard gauge, 4 feet 8½ inches, and operates about 1,315 miles. Its rails average 90 pounds, and it has no grades heavier than 2.6 per cent. The sharpest curves are around 10 degrees. This railroad is excellently operated, has a fine passenger train called the El Yaqui running every day in each direction from Guadalajara to Nogales, and is now completely dieselized.

I have been over this road several times and find it most interesting, with wonderful scenery along the barrancas and also along the Gulf Coast to Mazatlán.

Pacific Railroad of Mexico. Diesel freight train on the Miravalles

New Zealand

AS you go around the world you hear from all quarters that New Zealand and South Africa have the two best 3 foot 6 inch gauge railroads in the world. Because of an operation in 1953, I was unable to go to see the South African road which runs from Cape Town to Johannesburg, but I must say that I heartily agree that the New Zealand Government Railway is the best 3 foot 6 inch gauge road that I have seen anywhere in the world.

This New Zealand road when I was on it in 1949 was operated by a very attractive man and great railroader by the name of Frank Aickin. He had a grand record in World War II, having run the operating battalions in Egypt against Rommel, and he came out of it with a big name for himself. He was all over the United States in 1950 studying this country's electrification. The New Zealand road is now electrifying the main trunk, or main line as they call it, from Auckland to Frankton Junction and it is already electrified for 30 miles out of Wellington. In due course, the entire railroad probably will be. They have gotten a few diesels but, of course, there is no oil there and they simply do not want to bother with the labor problems connected with coal. They have to bring most of the coal used there from other countries. They are now, however, ordering more diesels.

It might be interesting to the American Brotherhoods to know that there is only one man on the electric engines on both passenger and freight service running out of Wellington. This, also, is a common practice in Switzerland in some districts. Of course, these engines all have the dead man's brake.

New Zealand, like Australia and Chile, has very good hardwood ties and they are not treated. Of course, New Zealand has magnificent forests and very, very good hardwood. This road has fine 80-pound rail. The bridges and drainage and all of the track are exceptional. They have a magnificent spiral in the middle of the main line between Auckland and Wellington which rises over a 2.5 per cent grade. They are very proud of that spiral. It reminded me of Tehachapi and that is the way they feel about it. There are seven tunnels in it. I rode the engine down on the Wellington Limited all night long and we went over that spiral at three o'clock in the morning under a full moon. Riding that wonderful little 4-8-4 with a 4-8-2 helper on this 3 foot 6 inch gauge road with eleven cars hauling about 400 tons is something I will always remember. The moon lighting the countryside really made a show. I thought of all the railroading I had done in other places so many thousands of miles away, and of the many moonlight nights I had ridden the mountains in so many other countries. I really got a bang out of it. These little engines have a terrific valve and when they are hooked up they talk back at you like the great Santa Fe 4-8-4's do. This Class K 4-8-4 type engine of theirs is the finest all-around piece of motive power of all the locomotives I have ridden on small gauge railroads. The majority burn oil. They have the Westinghouse brake equipment, roller bearings on all the axles, Walschaerts valve gear, and a maximum tractive effort of 32,740 pounds with a boiler pressure of 200 pounds. They had 56-inch drivers or as they put it, 4 feet 8 inches. They also had a fine 4-8-2 type engine Class J with a tractive effort of 26,520 pounds with a 200-pound boiler pressure and 54-inch driving wheels. Their workshops, as they are called there, were excellent and all their automatic signals were good wherever they had them. The tablet system for single lines was most interesting.

Never have I seen such enthusiastic people. I talked to some 450 of them in the Auckland Terminal one night. It simply amazed me what these fellows knew and the questions they asked, particularly about the American roads. They certainly know all about our railroads and a good many others in the world. One question was: Didn't the streamlined Pacific type engine that I had ridden in Australia remind me of the New Haven 4-6-4 type Class I-5, now scrapped? The cowling was the same, they said. That one really floored me. I sat there answering questions until well after midnight. They seemed to know all about my fishing. In fact, one paper had a front-page account headlined FROM FISH BOAT TO FOOT-PLATE.

In New Zealand they had what was to me a quaint trick of changing the entire engine crew, train crews and porters in the middle of the night at the meeting point of opposing trains—such as the Wellington Limited and the Auckland Limited—that had left their home terminals at the same time. Everybody unloaded way out of town and went back to the home terminal. Whether or not it is a good system I do not know, but they are doing it.

There are more roller bearings in New Zealand than in any other place I have ever seen in comparison to the amount of equipment they have, and believe it or not, I think that over 90 per cent of the suburban cars have roller bearings. They have very good steel coaches with Americanized leather seats; and if you feel like playing solitaire, a nice little shelf pulls down from the seat in front of you. The New Zealand railroad is lucky, and perhaps smart, not to have dining cars. Everybody gets out to have tea at every division point. As in many countries, the engine crews have their teapots right on the locomotive.

The enginemen, or drivers as they are called out there, are given two sets of overalls and one cap a year. The rest of their equipment they have to buy.

This road has no long engine runs and the engines rarely run through a division point. As with most government roads, there are not many railroad disputes between labor and management in New Zealand; but there was a lot of trouble about everything else and the general manager of the railroad had to go out and settle many things that were not related to the railroad business. While I was there I know that he was working on carpenters' strikes and milk strikes and it was,

152

so I was told, taking longer to load the ships in New Zealand than it took them to sail all the way to England.

The line on the South Island is also operated by the New Zealand Government Railways. This island is referred to as "The Switzerland Down Under." It is very beautiful. It has a particularly hot tunnel 5½ miles long which is electrified. This tunnel is named the Otira and boring was necessary to get around a 3 per cent grade.

The New Zealand Government Railways has some 625 steam locomotives and 1,530 passenger cars and around 32,000 freight cars. They are also modernized enough to put Centralized Traffic Control on some of the main lines and are extremely up and coming.

The sharpest curves in New Zealand are 17 degrees or 5 chains. Many roads keep their curves in chains and if you will divide the number of chains into the figure 85 you will get the degree of curvature. The heaviest grades are 6.7 per cent, which is 1 in 15 in the British language. One per cent is 1 in 100; 2 per cent, 1 in 50; 3 per cent, 1 in 33. On the amazing Rimutaka Incline there are seventeen-degree curves and 6 per cent grades. The Rimutaka Incline is now dieselized with lightweight diesel cars but will soon be electrified. I believe that steam operation is still used on heavy traffic days. This is considered to be one of the heaviest steam grades in any English-speaking country anywhere.

The Rimutaka Incline

The only remaining example of the "Fell" system of mountain traction at present in use on a steam-operated railway in any part of the world is owned by the New Zealand Government Railways. The original invention of this principle may be credited to Messrs. Vignoles and Ericson, England, who first patented it in 1830, but apparently it was perfected and re-patented by Mr. J. B. Fell in 1863. It was first used for commercial purposes in 1867, when a railway was built over the Mont Cenis Pass, connecting France and Italy.

Known as the Rimutaka Incline, the New Zealand section of Fell railways is 3 miles 7 chains in length, and is graded 1 in 15, with pinches as steep as 1 in 14. It abounds with 4-chain radius curves, and the longest section of straight track— facetiously known as "The Long Straight"—is less than one quarter mile in length. Three tunnels have been pierced, the longest of which is 649 yards in length. The Incline commences at Cross Creek, facing trains southbound to Wellington, and ascends to Summit, 1,141 feet above sea level. The climb, therefore, is no less than 869 feet in three miles. The railway from Wellington was completed as far as Featherston on October 12, 1878, when the section from Kaitoke to Featherston, over the rugged and formerly well-nigh impassable Rimutaka Mountains, was opened for traffic.

On the southern side of the Rimutakas the railway runs from Wellington to Upper Hutt, 19½ miles up the gradually ascending valley of the Hutt River, after which it climbs by means of steep gradients to Summit. The grades on this side of the mountain range are exceedingly heavy, being as steep as 1 in 35, uncompensated for curvature. Curves abound, and for the entire 14½ miles from Upper Hutt to Summit the railway is a succession of sharp 5-chain radius curves, many of which are check-railed.

The Fell system does not employ a cogged rack for traction but depends solely on adhesion, including that obtained on a large double-headed rail laid sideways between, and 6½ inches above, the running rails. This central grip rail is supported by brackets, which in turn are fastened to a heavy longitudinal timber bolted down to the transverse sleepers. The center-rail engine gear is housed between the frames of the locomotive and consists of four horizontal grip wheels which, controlled by means of a worm and wheel gearing operated by the fireman, are pressed tightly against the faces of the center rail. These grip wheels are held in position by powerful coil springs mounted in a cast steel frame. In addition to Westinghouse air brakes, special Fell brake gear is employed, consisting of four large cast-iron brake shoes which are brought to bear against the center rail. Special Fell brake vans are fitted with similar gear, these brakes being necessary to control the speed of descending trains.

Four 0-4-2(T) locomotives of the Fell type were built in 1875 by the Avonside Engine Co., England, to the design of a Swedish engineer named W. H. Widmark, these engines being already in operation when the line was opened for traffic. Classified "H," the four locomotives were named "Mont Cenis," "Mt. Cook," "Mt. Egmont," and "Mt. Tongariro."

When placed in service they had the following dimensions:

Weight in working trim	34½ tons
Diameter of coupled wheels	2 feet 8 inches
Cylinders: outside engine	14-in. dia. x 16-in. stroke
inside engine	12-in. dia. x 14-in. stroke
Working pressure	130 lb. per sq. in.
Tractive force	19,110 lb.
Grate area	13 sq. ft.
Capacity of side tanks	750 gals.
Capacity of bunker	10 cwt.

The Incline was operated by the four original locomotives until 1886, when two additional engines were built by Neilson & Co., Glasgow.

The later engines were modifications of their Avonside predecessors, but differed in certain respects, in addition to being somewhat heavier. Throughout the years, the Fell locomotives have been altered and reboilered to such an extent that there can be very little left of the original engines. They now weigh 40 tons in working trim, and are more powerful than when first built.

Despite their 70 years' service, the Fell locomotives are still rated to haul their maximum load of 65 tons up the 1 in 15 grade. The maximum load which may be hauled up the Incline by any one train is 250 tons, and the maximum speed during the descent is limited to 10 m.p.h.

From time to time, steam locomotives of other types have been used on the Rimutaka Incline. The first attempt to work the Incline with ordinary adhesion-type steam locomotives was made in 1902, when a small but powerful 2-6-2 tank engine of Class W was adapted for use. This was followed in 1903 by two powerful 4-6-4 tank locomotives of Class WE and, in 1905, by a large 2-6-6-0 compound tank engine of the Mallet type, Class E, which was specially built for service on the Rimutaka Incline. The latter locomotive was exceedingly powerful, and is believed to have hauled as much as 100 tons unassisted up the 1 in 15 grade. These four locomotives did not make use of the Fell center rail to assist them when climbing the grade, and although they proved quite successful when used in conjunction with Fell locomotives, the results obtained were not sufficiently good to warrant the replacement of the Fell engines with ordinary adhesion locomotives.

During the 71 years of its existence only one fatal train accident has occurred on the Rimutaka Incline. This disaster happened on September 11, 1880, when a train hauled by the Fell locomotive "Mt. Cook" was hurled by wind from the line at a point known as "Siberia," three passengers losing their lives. To combat the terrific gusts of wind which sweep down the mountainside at "Siberia," massive wooden breakwinds were erected, and these are still in existence.

An important development in the conveyance of passengers was the introduction of the petrol railcar in 1936, when these light vehicles, weighing 13½ tons, were placed in service on the Wairarapa-Wellington run, on which they are still employed. Their original 130 h.p. petrol engines have been replaced by 120 h.p. diesel engines which develop sufficient power to propel them up the Rimutaka Incline at a speed of 15 m.p.h. Seating 49 passengers, and capable of running at 60 m.p.h. over the comparatively level Wairarapa Plains, these railcars have reduced traveling time between Masterton and Wellington (66 miles) from 3½ hours to less than 2½ hours. Steam passenger trains, however, are still employed over this section during holiday rush periods.

Notwithstanding their advanced age, the Fell engines are still performing capably their daily task of moving traffic over what is probably the steepest section of steam-operated main line railway in the world. However, their death-knell has finally been sounded, for in spite of the many proposals throughout the years to replace them with other types of locomotives, the five-mile electrified tunnel which is to be bored through the mountains will solve for all time the problem of the Rimutaka Incline.

As the electric train tablet system is so interesting to railroad people throughout the world, especially in the United States, as is the staff system used on many British railroads and in other countries where roads were originally operated by the British (in fact in India they use tokens under somewhat the same system), I am including in this book four pages from Chapter 3 of the New Zealand Government Book of Rules which tells the story about this unique way of single track operation—or line operation as it is called there—when automatic signals are not in use. There are no train orders used. The readers can draw their own conclusions on the merits of this system. There is no doubt that it seems to be foolproof, and there has been very little trouble with it or with the staff either. However, there is a great deal of time taken in delivering and accepting the tablet and staff even though it is done in some countries, epecially in Chile, at speeds up to 50 miles per hour. The following description of the tablet system should give you a fairly clear idea of its principle.

Instructions and Regulations for Working Single-Line Railways by the Electric Train Tablet System

Whenever the term "Officer-in-charge" is used in these Regulations it must be understood to mean the Stationmaster, Signalman, or other member who is in charge of the Tablet Apparatus for the time being, and he only is authorized to receive and deliver the Tablets, and remove them from or place them in the Apparatus. No Cadet or Junior Porter is to be permitted to work the Block except in cases where the written authority of the District Manager is first obtained.

Object of the Electric Train Tablet System

The object of the Electric Train Tablet Signalling is to prevent more than one Train being between any two Tablet Stations at the same time, and, when no Train is in the Section between the Tablet Stations, to admit of a Train being started from either end.

This is accomplished by every Train carrying a Tablet, one Tablet only being obtainable from the Tablet Instruments of the same Section at the same time.

The construction of the Apparatus is so based upon the Interlocking principle that the Train Tablet itself is the key to the whole plan, and it renders the issue of the Train Tablet absolutely safe at either end of a Section, and under the sole control of the Station to which the Train is approaching.

No Train Tablet can be issued from Station "Y" without the consent and co-operation of Station "Z"; and when once a Station has issued a Train Tablet no other Tablet can be obtained for the same Section until the one issued has been delivered at its destination and placed in the Instrument, or reinserted in the Instrument from which it was withdrawn.

The Crossing-place of a Train can be altered immediately with perfect safety.

The Signalling of Trains on the Electric Train Tablet System does not in any way dispense with the use of Fixed, Hand, or Fog Signals, whenever or wherever such Signals may be requisite to protect Obstructions on the Line.

Normal Position of Instruments

When the Tablet Instruments are not in use the words "Line Closed" are shown on the screens, and the Needle Indicators are in the vertical position.

Custody and Transference of Tablet

Except as provided in Regulation 23, the Officer-in-charge of the Tablet Working for the time being is the sole member authorized to take a Tablet from or place it in the Instrument; or to receive the Tablet from and deliver it to the Engine-driver: provided, however, that the Member in charge of the Tablet Working may, in exceptional cases, specially appoint a member of the Station Staff, duly qualified to act, and delegate to such Member the duty of delivering the Tablet to and receiving it from the Engine-driver. The Member so appointed will be held responsible for the safe custody of the Tablet given him, and for the prompt and proper discharge of the duty assigned to him. The Engine-driver, while the Tablet is in his charge, must carry it in the socket or other place provided for the purpose. Under no circumstances, except as provided in Regulations 10, 27 and 27A, must a Tablet be transferred from one Train to another without being passed through the Instrument and dealt with in accordance with these Regulations.

The number of the Tablet carried by each Train must be entered in the Train-Register book.

Engine-Driver not to Start without Tablet and Proper Signals Being Exhibited

(*a*) Except as provided in Regulations 27A, 28, and 31, an Engine-driver will render himself liable to dismissal if he leaves a Tablet Station without the Tablet for that Section of the Line over which he is about to run, or unless it has been shown to him as required by the following paragraph, and by Regulation 18.

(*b*) When a Train is drawn by more than one Engine, the Tablet must be shown to each Engine-driver, and be delivered to and carried by the Engine-driver of the Leading Engine. When two or more Light Engines are coupled together, the Tablet must be shown to each Engine-driver, and be delivered to and carried by the Engine-driver of the last Engine.

(*c*) After receiving the Tablet the Engine-driver must not proceed until all the necessary Fixed or other Signals have been exhibited. He must keep the Tablet under his own charge (except as explained in Regulations 27, 27A and 34) until he reaches the end of the Section, when he must give it up to the Officer-in-Charge.

The Tablet is an indication that the Line is clear only to the Home Signal at the Station or Junction in advance, and Engine-drivers must regulate the speed of their Trains accordingly.

(*d*) Engine-drivers must be extremely careful not to take the Tablet beyond the Station at which it ought to be left.

(*e*) Engine-drivers must reduce the speed of their Trains to fifteen miles per hour when passing a Tablet Station at which they are not timed to stop, so as to admit of their safely delivering and receiving the Train Tablet but where Automatic Tablet Exchangers are fitted the speed need not be reduced.

(*f*) The Officer-in-charge of the Tablet Working will render himself liable to severe punishment should he contribute to any irregularity in the Tablet Working.

(*g*) Each Tablet has engraved or marked on it the name of the Tablet Station at each end of the Section to which it applies, and the Tablets of adjoining Sections are different in shape.

Working Fixed Signals

(*a*) When Trains which have to cross each other are approaching a Station from opposite directions or from converging Lines, and the Signals have to be lowered for one Train, they must not be lowered for the other Train until the First Train has come to a dead stop, and the Signalman has seen that the Line on which the other Train will arrive has been left quite clear.

(*b*) Where Starting Signals or Advanced Starting Signals are provided, except in the cases referred to in Regulations 27, 27A, 28, and 31, the Starting Signal or the Advanced Starting Signal must not be lowered until a Tablet has been obtained for the Train to proceed to the Tablet Station in advance.

Normal Position of Fixed Signals

The "Danger" Signal must always be kept exhibited at all the Fixed Signals at Tablet Stations, except when it is necessary to lower or turn them off for a Train to pass; and before any Signal is lowered or turned off care must be taken to ascertain that the Line on which the Train is about to run is Clear, and that these and other Regulations have been duly complied with.

Description of the Tablet Instrument

The Apparatus consists essentially of a slide, "R"; a bell-plunger, "B"; a switch-plunger, "C"; a slide, "S"; a visual signal, "V," showing three positions—"Line closed," "Up Train approaching" or "Down Train approaching," and "Up Train on Line" or "Down Train on Line"; a slot, "T"; and an indicator, "I."

The slide "R" is for the purpose of inserting Tablets into the Apparatus, and can be withdrawn at will.

The bell-plunger serves to transmit all signals on the bells, as per code.

The switch-plunger "C" is for the purpose of switching the current into electro-magnets to unlock slide "S."

The slide "S" is kept locked, and cannot be withdrawn without the consent and cooperation of the member at the distant cabin, and the Visual Signals as per code have been exchanged.

The slot "T" shows the Tablets in cylinder of apparatus.

The indicator "I" indicates all outgoing and incoming signals sent on the bell-plunger from either end.

Regulations for Working Single-Line Railways by the Train Staff and Ticket System

The object of the train staff and ticket system is to prevent more than one train being between any two train-staff stations at the same time, and, when no train is in the section between the train-staff stations, to admit of a train being started from the end at which the train staff is located. This is accomplished by each train carrying a train staff or staff ticket, in accordance with the regulations contained herein.

The signalling of trains under the train staff and ticket system does not in any way dispense with the use of fixed, hand, or detonator signals when or where such signals may be necessary.

The rules, instructions contained in the working time-tables, and other printed or written notices, will be effective so far as they are applicable to the train staff and ticket system.

1. Description and Custody of Staff and Staff Tickets

(a) Each staff has engraved upon it the name of the station at each end of the section to which the staff applies.

(b) The staff boxes and staff tickets for the different sections are different in colouring, and the staffs of adjoining sections are different in shape.

(c) All staff ticket books at a station must be kept in the appropriate staff ticket box, the key to open the box being the staff for the same section as that for which the box is provided, so that, the box being kept locked (for which the Member in charge of staff working is responsible), tickets cannot be obtained unless the staff for the section is available to unlock the box.

(d) Only one staff ticket must be taken from the staff ticket box at the one time. The box must be locked after each ticket is taken out, and must not be opened again until it is necessary to obtain another ticket for a following train.

(e) Staff tickets must be issued in the order of their progressive numbers, after being duly filled in and signed by the Member in charge of staff working. Engine-drivers must satisfy themselves that tickets are properly filled in.

(f) All spare staff tickets which cannot be kept in the staff ticket box must be locked away by the Officer in Charge at the station, who is responsible for their safe custody.

(g) The staff, when at the station, must not be kept in the staff ticket box, but on the brackets on the outside of it.

(h) The Member in charge of staff working for the time being is the sole member authorized to receive or deliver a staff or staff ticket at a train-staff station.

2. Every Train To Carry Staff or Staff Ticket

(a) A staff or a staff ticket must be carried on the leading engine of each train. A train must not be permitted to start from a station with a staff ticket unless the staff for that portion of the line over which it is to travel is then at the starting station, except in accordance with these regulations or as may be authorized by the Officer Controlling Train-running.

After receiving the staff or staff ticket, an Engine-driver must not start the train until the necessary fixed or other signals have been exhibited. The staff or staff ticket does not authorize a train to pass fixed signals at "Stop."

(b) When a train which is ready to start from a station will not be followed by another train before a train will leave the station at the other end of the section, the Member in charge of staff working must give the staff to the Engine-driver of the waiting train.

After the staff has been sent away, no other train may follow in the same direction until the staff for that section has been returned.

On arrival of the train at the other end of the section, the staff must be immediately collected by the Member in charge of staff working; it will then be available for the next train which will travel through the section.

The Engine-driver receiving the staff on an engine must place it in the staff socket, when provided.

(c) If two or more trains are required to travel in the same direction before a staff can be returned, the Member in charge of staff working must furnish the Engine-driver of each train not accompanied by the staff with a Mis. 28 staff ticket (see specimen on page 170) properly filled in and signed, the staff for the section being shown to him at the same time.

The Engine-driver must not accept the staff ticket unless at the same time he sees the staff in the possession of the Member in charge of staff working.

The staff must be given to the Engine-driver of the last train.

A staff ticket will apply only to a single journey to the other end of the section, where it must be immediately collected by the Member in charge of staff working, who must write the word "Cancelled" across the face of it. Cancelled tickets must be forwarded to the District Traffic Manager at the close of business on each Saturday.

(d) Where communication by telegraph or telephone exists, the arrival of each train unaccompanied by the staff must be reported to the Officer in Charge at the other end of the section, and the Member in charge of staff working must not despatch another train until he has been advised that the preceding train has arrived.

(e) Where communication by telegraph or telephone does not exist, and unless the Officer in Charge can ascertain that the section is clear, or special authority has been received from the Officer Controlling Train-running, a train must not be allowed to follow another train until the ordinary running-time of the section has elapsed, and the Engine-driver has been advised of the nature and departure-time of the preceding train.

(f) Where communication by telegraph or telephone does not exist, intermediate sidings may be worked only by a train which is accompanied by the staff.

(g) The speed of trains must be reduced sufficiently to enable the staff or staff ticket to be exchanged with safety, and to enable the Engine-driver to satisfy himself that he has received the proper authority to enter the section.

(*h*) An Engine-driver must not set his train back unless he is in possession of the staff.

3. Shunting Outside Home Signals.

An engine must not foul the single line outside a Home signal for shunting purposes unless the Engine-driver is in possession of the staff, or unless he receives the authority of the Officer in Charge, who must not give such authority unless the staff is held at his end of the section.

4. Crossing Trains.

A train must not pass or cross another train except at a train-staff station.

5. Work Trains.

(*a*) A work train must not stop to work in a section unless the Engine-driver is in possession of the staff.

(*b*) A staff ticket must not be issued for a work train which is required to work in a section.

(*c*) When a work train is to return to the train-staff station in the rear, shunting outside the Home signal at that end of the station must not be permitted until the work train has cleared the section.

(*d*) The Engine-driver of a work train which is required to work in a section must be told when receiving the staff to which end of the section it is to be taken, and the time at which it must be there in order to clear the section for the next train.

(*e*) If the Guard of a work train should require his train to return to the train-staff station in the rear instead of going through to the train-staff station in advance, he must obtain permission to return from the Officer in Charge before the train enters the section.

6. Working Trains On Each Side of An Obstruction.

If an accident or obstruction should occur and traffic is likely to be stopped for a considerable time, the following special arrangements must be made for the working of trains to and from the train-staff station on each side of the point of obstruction:—

(*a*) **If the accident or obstruction should occur when a train is on the section,** so that the train is disabled and cannot be removed from the section by the train engine, the staff must be retained to work trains between the point of obstruction and the station on the side from which the Guard, after conferring with the Engine-driver, decides it is more convenient to use the staff; on the other side, trains must be worked by a Pilotman.

The following procedure must be adopted:—

(i) The Guard must place the Engine-driver in charge of the point of obstruction, and after obtaining from him the written undertaking referred to in Rule 73 (*d*), must himself go to the end of the section where the staff will not be used, and arrange for pilot working to be instituted;

(ii) When pilot working has been instituted and the Pilotman is satisfied that arrangements are understood, trains may be allowed to travel between the train-staff station and the point of obstruction, under the control and by the permission of the Pilotman;

(iii) The Engine-driver in charge of the point of obstruction must hand the staff (together with the written undertaking referred to in subclause (i) hereof) to the Fireman, and instruct him to take it to the station from which trains will be worked by staff to the point of obstruction;

(iv) If the train is travelling with a staff ticket instead of the staff, the Fireman must take the staff ticket (together with the written undertaking) to the station where it was issued and hand it to the Member in charge of staff working, who must cancel it. The staff must then be issued for the working of trains in accordance with the preceding subclause;

(v) The Engine-driver in charge of the point of obstruction will be responsible for seeing that the necessary protection is maintained until employees are specially appointed to take charge of the obstruction;

(vi) When the line is again clear and safe for traffic, the staff has been given up to the Officer in Charge, and Pilot working cancelled, normal staff and ticket working may be resumed;

(vii) A train must not be allowed to pass the point where the obstruction existed without a staff or staff ticket, and the Pilotman must accompany the first train carrying a staff or staff ticket through the section;

(viii) When an obstruction occurs away from a train-staff station, the staff must not be placed on the staff ticket box at either end of the obstructed section until the line is again clear and safe for traffic.

(*b*) **If the accident or obstruction should occur when a train is not on the section,** the Officers in Charge at both ends of the section must confer and appoint a competent member to take charge of the point of obstruction, and for Pilotmen to be appointed to work trains between the obstruction and the station on each side of it until the line is again clear.

When the line is again clear and safe for traffic, and pilot working has been cancelled, normal staff and ticket working may be resumed.

The Pilotmen must accompany the first train carrying a staff or staff ticket over the portions of the section where they have respectively been acting as Pilotmen.

(*c*) In each instance, the necessary protection must be maintained until the line is again clear.

7. Portion Of Train Left On A Section.

(*a*) If a portion of a train should be left on a section, owing to an accident or to the inability of the engine to take the whole of the train forward, and it becomes necessary for the engine to return to the rear portion of the train from the train-staff station in advance, the Engine-driver must retain possession of the staff or staff ticket until the whole of the train has been removed from the section.

If, however, the train engine is not to be used to remove the rear portion of the train, the Engine-driver, upon receiving written instructions from the Officer Controlling Train-running, must deliver the staff or staff ticket to the Officer in Charge, who will arrange for the line to be cleared.

(*b*) If the Engine-driver is in possession of the staff, the engine may return for the rear portion of the train without the Engine-driver holding written instructions from the Guard authorizing him to do so.

(*c*) If the Engine-driver is in possession of a staff ticket, he must not return for the rear portion of the train unless he holds written instructions from the Guard authorizing him to do so; the note from the Guard to the Engine-driver must also state that the train is protected.

8. Engine Disabled Between Two Staff Stations.

(*a*) If an engine carrying a staff should become disabled between two stations, the Engine-driver must hand the staff (together with the written undertaking referred to in Rule 73 (*d*)) to the Fireman, and instruct him to take it to the station from which assistance is more likely to be obtained.

The Fireman of the disabled engine must not allow the staff to pass out of his possession until he hands it to the Engine-driver of a relief engine, and he must accompany the relief engine to the disabled train, advising the Engine-driver where and under what circumstances the disabled train is situated. The Engine-driver of the relief engine must not allow the staff to pass out of his possession until the whole of the disabled train has been removed from the section, when he must deliver the staff to the Member in charge of staff working at either end of the section.

(*b*) If the engine is travelling with a staff ticket instead of the staff, the Fireman must take the staff ticket (together with the written undertaking) to the station where it was issued, and hand it to the Member in charge of staff working, who must cancel the ticket. The staff must then be issued for delivery to the Engine-driver of the relief engine.

(*c*) In each instance, the necessary protection must be maintained until the line is again clear.

9. Lost Or Damaged Staff

(*a*) If a staff should be lost, or so damaged that it will not open the staff ticket boxes, the Officers in Charge at both ends of the section must communicate with each other and make arrangements to institute pilot working.

When the staff has been found or repaired or a relieving staff and boxes have been supplied, pilot working may be cancelled.

When a staff is damaged and will not open the staff ticket boxes, the Pilotman must take possession of the damaged staff and keep it securely locked up.

(*b*) If a missing staff is found, it must be handed to the Officer in Charge at the station at which pilot working was instituted, who must make arrangements for normal working to be resumed. Before the regular staff and staff ticket boxes are brought into use, the relieving staff and boxes must be withdrawn and forwarded to the member who is responsible for their safe custody.

10. Method Of Instituting And Working Under Pilot Working.

Unless inconsistent with the context, the method of instituting, working under, and cancelling pilot working will be in accordance with the regulations for working single-line railways by the electric train tablet system.

Interior of the New Zealand Government Railroad's two-berth sleeping car compartment with berth made up for the night.

F. W. Aickin, then General Manager of the New Zealand Government Railways, stands between Mr. and Mrs. S. Kip Farrington, Jr., as he meets them on their arrival at Wellington. Note the good-looking leather-bound New Zealand Railways operating timetable the author is holding and also the dirt on his face. He has been riding the locomotive all night and not sleeping in a commodious compartment like the one above.

A tablet instrument of the patent used by New Zealand Railways. This particular machine and its counterpart at the next station with which it is electrically interlocked governs the passage of trains over the 3.9 miles of single track between Linton and Longburn, a typical section of the Wellington-Auckland line.

As no tablet is in use, the instrument is shown in its normal position of "line closed." Clearly visible through the glazed slot above the lowest side are the rounded edges of several tablets. On the left is the train register and below it is the open circuit telephone which enables the station agent to speak instantly to the train control operator, the New Zealand equivalent of train dispatcher, at Wellington.

Hauled by a light Pacific type locomotive of Class A, this Wellington-bound freight train approaches the exchange post at Paraparaumu where the station agent has placed an empty tablet sling onto the trip arm of the automatic exchanger. The train which is approaching from the north will drop a Waikanae-Paraparaumu tablet onto the spear-shaped jaw above. As the remaining 30.2 miles into Wellington are protected by automatic signals and for 26.3 miles of this mileage by CTC, a fresh tablet will not be required. The train must, however, pick up the empty sling in order that the exchanger will trip and so swing clear of the cars.

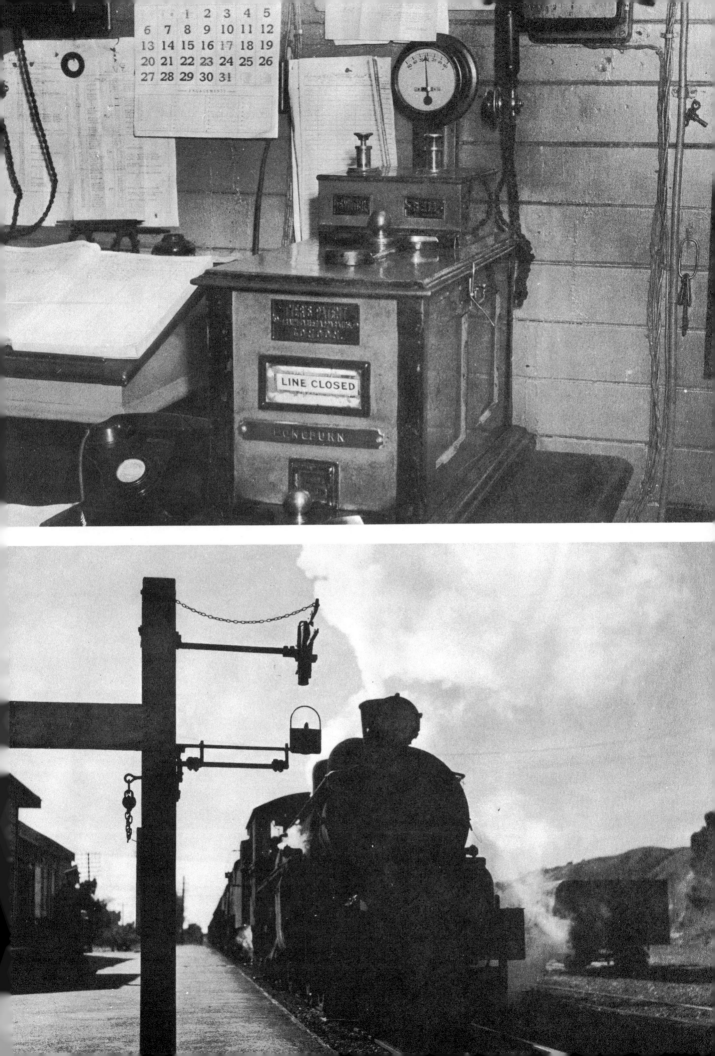

Here the exchange is about to take place. Note the snappy cap the engine driver wears.

The trip mechanism of the automatic tablet exchanger. As the train collects the tablet, the impact turns the rod on which the tablet is mounted. This displaces the cam which in turn allows the spring-loading retaining catch to disengage from the iron frame of the receiving arm which a powerful coil spring swings clear of the train.

The exchange has been made and the engineer will now take the empty sling from the exchanger arm which also will be removed and stowed in the cab. Had the engineer been entering another tablet section instead of an automatic signal area, the sling would have contained a tablet.

The station agent removes the sling containing the Waikanae-Paraparaumu tablet which now will be placed in the Paraparaumu tablet instrument. After this has been done, the correct bell signal is given and switch plunger movements made. The circuit will be cleared and both machines left free for the issue of another tablet.

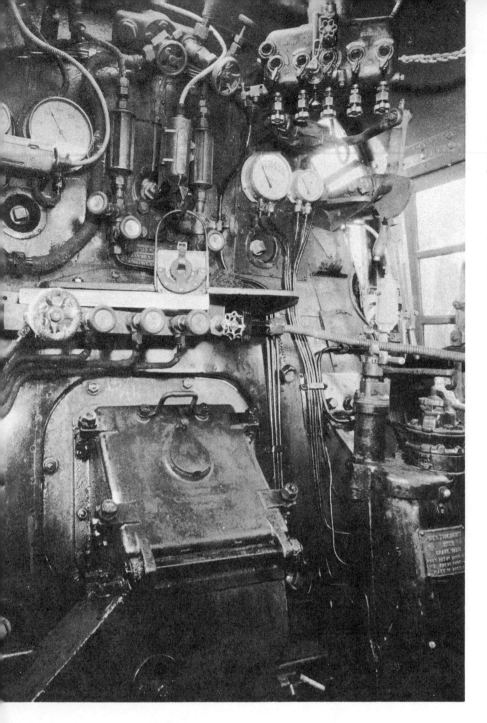

Here's where they hang the tablet sling on the boiler back head of their great oil-fired 4-8-4 type Class KA locomotive. Note the special hook under the water glasses lamp. Note the Westinghouse pedestal type ET brake equipment, Detroit sight feed lubricator, front end throttle, power reverse gear. Quite amazing for a 3 foot 6 inch gauge locomotive.

The tablet itself. Here is one used between Wellington and Rongatai. Note the number and the type of cutting in it. Each tablet has a different cutting so that there will never be any danger of one of them getting into the wrong machine. They will only fit the machine to which they are assigned.

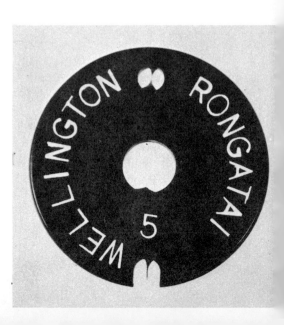

The 3.00 P.M. Wellington Express awaiting the departure signal from Auckland's fine modern terminal. In New Zealand, they call the road engine a "train engine,"—their semi-streamlined Class J 4-8-2 type is shown here—and they call the helper engine a "pilot"—here a coal-burning Class K 4-8-4. Note trucks of roller bearing suburban coach to right of leading engine.

Southbound freight train crossing the 258-foot-high Makatote Viaduct behind a low wheel 4-8-2 Class X situated near Hakaune. This is the highest viaduct on the Welling-on-Auckland main line. The typical 30-foot brake van or caboose at the rear is one of 290 standard brake vans built between 1889 and 1942 for the New Zealand Railway. The oldest were of wood while the latest are of steel construction. They are employed on both freight and local passenger trains as required. This is a very fine type of American caboose as compared to the brake vans found on most foreign railroads. Notice the covered wagons in the train and how many of the cars are 4-wheeled; also the fine New Zealand

Photograph of the Royal Train operated for HRH the Duke of Gloucester in 1934 ascending the 6.7 per cent grade of the Rimutaka Incline. The heavy train necessitated the use of five of the six special 0-4-2 Fell-type center-rail-gripping locomotives. In the distance of 3 miles the railroad climbs 869 feet in height.

Train arriving at Avon Creek at the bottom of the Rimutaka Incline. Note the end of the center rail and the sign marking the beginning. The number "5" means that the curve ahead is a 5-chain curve. The New Zealand Railroad is very well marked. In this author's opinion every good railroad should be well marked.

Train ascending the Rimutaka Incline. This is the spot where the train referred to earlier was blown over in 1880.

(*Photo by W. W. Stewart.*)

A typical New Zealand mixed train #107 with a Class AB locomotive 4-6-2 type passing Aorangi.   (*Photo by W. W. Stewart*)

Train #133 the Auckland-Rotorua Express with Class K and AB locomotives coupled running along the Auckland waterfront.
(*Photo by W. W. Stewart*)

View from the deck, or "foot-plate" to the New Zealanders, coming into the Auckland Terminal. Note the automatic signals and the shunting engine. (*Photo by W. W. Stewart*)

The 3:40 P.M. Auckland-Papakura train #191 with Class J 4-8-2 type locomotive coming out of the Parnell Tunnel. (*Photo by W. W. Stewart*)

Type of first-class coach used on the long distance runs by the New Zealand Government Railways with the North American type of seating. The walls and ceilings are lined with green and silver rexine. Note the large windows.

Close-up of the four-position reclining chair in the New Zealand 56-foot first-class coaches. Note the shelves and ashtrays on the backs of the seats.

Invercargill-Christchurch (South Island) Express skirting the shore before beginning its northward climb over the rugged coastal hills between Dunedin and the broad plains of Canterbury, South Island, New Zealand. The road engine is a Class AB Pacific 4-6-2 with a Class J 4-8-2 type helper.

Goods train hauled by 2-8-4 electric locomotive Class ED about to enter the first of two long tunnels which carry the Wellington-Auckland main trunk railway beneath the hills surrounding Wellington Harbor, which may be seen in the background. Opened in 1937, this 8½ mile deviation with 1 per cent grades replaced the original main line connection from Wellington with its 3 per cent climb and seven tunnels in less than as many miles. The Wellington-Paekariki section of 24½ miles was electrified at 1,500 volts DC in 1940. The small board marked "20" indicates the curve of 20 chains radius requiring a reduction of speed to 45 miles an hour. Paralleling the harbor highway may be seen the two tracks of the Hutt Valley Railway which after passing through extensive suburbs climbs over the Rimutaka Mountains on the famous incline to the northern farmlands.

Right side of the New Zealand Government Railways' great 4-8-4 type heavy duty locomotive Class K. Between 1932 and 1937, thirty of those engines were built at Hutt workshops. They are used for heavy freight and express train haulage on the North Island; 17 have been converted to oil. Thirty-three more, called Class A, were built between 1939 and 1945 and are also used only on the North Island. Thirty-one of these burn oil and the only differences among Class A and K and KA is that the latter is 7 tons heavier in weight. Two later engines were built having roller-bearing rods as well as roller bearings on all the wheels and these also have Baker Valve Gear.

These engines weigh in working order	137 tons
Adhesive weight	53 tons
Length overall	70 ft.
Diameter of driving wheels	4 ft. 6 in. or 54 in.
Cylinders	20 x 26 in.
Boiler pressure	200 lbs. per sq. in.
Tractive force at 80% boiler pressure	30,815 lbs.
Combined heating surface	2,418 sq. ft.
Grate area	47.7 sq. ft.

They are equipped with Walschaert's Valve Gear, power reverse gear, feed water heaters, twin air pumps and roller bearings on all the axles and the coal burners have air operated fire doors.

This locomotive the author considers the finest steam locomotive he has ever ridden on for other than standard gauge outside the U.S. and he compares it favorably with many standard gauge steam locomotives he has ridden.

Left side of Class K 4-8-4 type locomotive.

New Zealand Government's Class JA 4-8-2 type. Thirty-five of these locomotives are in service in the South Island, having been built at the Hillside Workshops at Dunedin, and 10 of the Class J built in Scotland in 1939 are in service on the North Island.

They weigh in working trim	109 tons
Adhesive weight	44 tons
Length overall	66 ft. 9 in.
Diameter of driving wheels	4 ft. 6 in.
Cylinders	18 x 26 in.
Boiler pressure	200 lbs. per sq. in.
Tractive force at 80% boiler pressure	24,920 lbs.
Heating surface	1,752 sq. ft.
Grate area	39 sq. ft.

Looking at the famous Raurimu Spiral just north of National Park, New Zealand. This is a great engineering feat and with only a 2 per cent grade, spirals and tunnels have reduced the climb by many feet. It is one of the most interesting pieces of railroad construction over which the author has ever ridden.

Fast goods train hauled by Class K locomotive 4-8-4 type coming
into Patakura.   (*Photo by W. W. Stewart*)

Australia

THERE are six different railroads in Australia and the author has ridden four of them: the New South Wales, the South Australia, the Victoria, and the Queensland, over which the trains of the New South Wales are run a few miles into Brisbane on standard gauge. The six roads in this wonderful country have five different gauges. The South Australia has 1,475 miles of 5 feet 3 inches and the Victoria 4,634 miles. The Commonwealth Road has 1,100 miles of standard 4 feet 8½ inches; the New South Wales, 6128 miles; while the Queensland has only 69 miles. The Commonwealth has 1,075 miles of 3 feet 6 inches; the Queensland, 6,447 miles; the South Australia, 1,067 miles; the Western Australia, 4,348 miles. The Victoria has 114 miles of 2 feet 6 inches, and the Queensland has 30 miles of 2 feet. This gives the reader a small picture of the enormity of the Australian operation with their various gauges and, believe me, it is a big undertaking to transfer all express, baggage, mail, freight, and passengers at points where the break of gauge occurs.

The Australians are good railroaders, have some excellent track, and their hardwood ties, like those in Chile and New Zealand, do not need treating. However, they use many British practices, the staff system on single line with ticket as well as left-hand operation and left-hand running.

The Commonwealth Railroad has a 4-6-0 type of locomotive bought from the New York, New Haven and Hartford Railroad. There were three different classes of 4-8-4 type in operation there during my stay and three different classes of mountain-type 4-8-2 locomotives. Diesels are now taking over and even with the amount of coal in New South Wales, I do not believe it will be long before the entire continent is dieselized. Paul W. Johnston, who is now President of the Erie Railroad in the United States, was in command of the railroad battalions there during the war and is spoken of very highly by everyone as one of so many of our railroad officials who did such magnificent jobs where they were stationed. Wherever one goes, one hears nothing but praise for the officers and men of our railroad operating battalions in World War II.

The author rode the New South Wales road from Brisbane to Albury, with several intermediate trips from Sydney to Newcastle; the Victoria Road from Albury to Melbourne and Melbourne to Adelaide, the last few miles being over the South Australia road.

New South Wales RR 4-8-2 type Class D-57 with a wheat train at Wallendbeen. Notice all the four-wheel wagons. Almost all the freight cars in England and Australia, as well as many of the other foreign countries, do not have 4-wheel trucks, or bogies, as the British call them.

Newcastle Express near Mullet Creek and the Hawksbury River. This is the main line of the road between Sydney and Brisbane and there are five of these 7-car trains like the above with good fast turn-around service on the 150-mile run. The heaviest grade between these two important cities was 2 per cent.

he dieselized "Silver City Comet" of the New South Wales Rail-
ad which is air conditioned and operates three times a week
tween Parks and Broken Hill, 421 miles in each direction.

The most powerful steam locomotive in Australia—the New South
Wales 4-8-2 type Class D-57 used in goods service. These engines are stoker fired, have 60-inch driving wheels, 200-pound
boiler pressure, and exert a tractive effort of 56,000 pounds. The
tank capacity is 9,000 Imperial gallons and they carry 14 tons
of coal. They were built in 1929 and 1930. They have three
cylinders and the Australians experience the same difficulties in
maintaining them as the United States roads did with their 3-
cylinder steam locomotives.

The new Hawksbury River railway bridge between Sydney and Newcastle. This bridge is the most important in all of Australia and carries the heaviest traffic. It was also the most important in World War II, as it carried the traffic to Brisbane and points north, and Newcastle is the Pittsburgh of Australia. They say that every Japanese plane that was shot down during the war anywhere near Australia had a map of this bridge in it or on the pilot. If this bridge had been put out of service, there would have been no detouring except by ship and they were at a premium during the war. I can think of no comparable place in the United States where this could have occurred. It was also said that the few Japanese submarines that shelled Australia had this bridge in mind.

The fine 4-6-2 type New South Wales Class C-38 locomotive used in passenger service on all their crack trains. They have 69-inch wheels, a boiler pressure of 245 pounds, and tractive effort of 36,200 pounds. Their tenders carry 8,100 imperial gallons and 14 tons of coal. Twenty-five of them are not streamlined.

This is the crack Spirit of Progress, one of the few streamlined trains in Australia, which is operated by the Victorian Government Railways from Melbourne to Albury, where passengers change trains because of the difference in the gauges to continue on to Sydney. This train carries one of the few dining cars in Australia and the author rode this streamlined Pacific-type engine from Melbourne to Albury and then continued on the New South Wales locomotive all night into Sydney. The Australians, who have a great sense of humor and are fine kidders, call this train the "Spirit of Salts," which gives them a great laugh.

Sydney Railroad Station of the New South Wales Road showing the lines leading into the city underground railroad, which carries some of them beneath the streets of this fine city. The late Prime Minister Chiefley, who was in office when I visited Australia, was a former engine driver and had eighteen years of service. He sent for me, relieving me of all of the United States railroad books that I had with me. I have never been in any country that appreciates what the United States did for them in World War II more than the Australians. I have never received greater hospitality anywhere where I have fished or railroaded than from these sport-loving people who play and excel in so many sports. Their beaches have no superior for surfing, and when I arrived there I had 54 wires of welcome, many from people whom, of course, I did not know.

Union of South Africa

THE South African Railways, with the New Zealand Government Railways, are considered the best 3 foot 6 inch gauge railways in the world. This railroad operates 13,371 miles of line, of which 12,578 are 3 foot 6 inch gauge and 793 miles are 2 foot gauge. There are 621 miles electrified with 3,000 volt D.C. overhead-wire operation. They own 2,400 steam locomotives of 3 foot 6 inch gauge and 65 for the 2 foot gauge and have 260 electric locomotives in service. They own more than 75,000 freight cars, and 4,100 passenger cars are in service.

The road gets a good average haul per ton, it being around 250 miles, and as there are practically no river systems and the highways are bad, they carry an amazing number of passengers per year, around 250 million. The majority of the tonnage haul is coal and coke, which accounts for about 32 per cent of the total business; other minerals and ores, 16 per cent; products of farms, 20 per cent; fertilizers, 3 per cent; and heavy goods like machinery, 12 per cent; heavy building materials, 6 per cent; and lumber, 3 per cent.

The road is dispatched on single line with the electric train tablet and staff systems, and on the double track sections by the lock and block system, and, of course, the working timetables. They have good signaling and their standard rail on the main line averages from 81 to 95 pounds per yard. The maximum curvature is 19 degrees and the heaviest grades are 3 per cent. The line reaches a height of 6,871 feet above sea level on the Belfast–Steelport line. Their longest continuing grade, between Durban and Pietermaritzburg, is 19 miles, with 1.5 per cent ruling grade and 11 degree curves. The maximum running speed is 55 miles an hour. They have more than 40,000 bridge openings, of which 10,000 are regarded as major bridges. They have a great deal of trouble with high water and severe flooding as the rainfall is heavy. The road's longest steel bridge is 3,514 feet across the Orange River and their longest double-track tunnel is the Delville Tunnel, which is 3,002 feet long. There is also a single-track tunnel 3,202 feet in length. They have two crack passenger trains which are known throughout the world—the Blue Train which operates from Johannesburg to Cape Town, 956 miles, in 26 hours and averages about 695 tons in weight. It is hauled by steam locomotives except in the Johannesburg Terminal district and all of the steam engines are fired by coal. This train operates twice a week. It is painted blue and cream with gold lining and aluminum roof. Their other famous train is the Orange Express, operating between Durban and Cape Town, 1,301 miles, and covering the distance in 42 hours and 50 minutes. The average tonnage is 545 tons. This train is also hauled by steam locomotives except from Durban to Harrismith on the electrified portion of that line. It also operates twice a week and is painted with cream and maroon. These fine passenger trains carry dining cars, salon cars and are first class in every respect.

Vacuum brakes are used on all the locomotives and cars and the road has some very excellent examples of modern steam locomotives. They have 124 Pacific-type locomotives and 1,271 various design mountain-type 4-8-2 locomotives and one 2-10-4-type locomotive. They have a half dozen 4-8-4 types and, of course, a considerable number of Garretts. This road adequately serves the great Union of South Africa and is expertly operated by a fine staff of all-around engineers, railroaders, and mechanical experts.

The Blue Train hauled by Class 23 4-8-2 type locomotive, which has a tractive effort of 28,816 pounds, 63-inch wheels and a boiler pressure of 225 pounds. Its tender has a water capacity of 9,500 imperial gallons and 18 tons of coal.

The Orange Express crossing the Berg River in the Cape Province hauled by Class 23 4-8-2 type locomotive.

South African Railways' locomotive of the same class pictured below—a condensing engine.

South African Railways' 4-8-4 type non-condensing locomotive Class 25.

atest class of 4-8-2 mountain-type locomotive in South Africa.
hey are 15F with a tractive power of 27,844 pounds, 60-inch
heels and a boiler pressure of 200 pounds. The tender has a
ater capacity of 6,000 imperial gallons and carries 14 tons of
al.

Blue Train leaving Johannesburg hauled by Class 3E electric
locomotive with a tractive effort of 34,500 pounds. These electric engines have air brakes on the locomotives. Note the multiple unit cars and steam locomotives in the background standing
in the Johannesburg coach yards. Also note the Blue Train's
insignia on the head end of the electric locomotive.

East Africa

I HAVE never been to East Africa or had the chance to ride the East African Railways but Mrs. Farrington ably represented me while I was fishing in Peru in September, 1952. She met all the officials and rode some of their locomotives and trains. She brought me back much data on the roads, including the reports from the Commissioner for Transport, and photographs.

The East African road climbs to 9,000 feet above sea level at its highest point and has many miles of grades from 1 to 4 per cent but the curvature is not too bad, the worst being about 10 degrees.

It has also been my great misfortune not to have been able to visit South Africa to ride their fine railroad which ranks with the New Zealand Government Railways as being one of the best 3 foot 6 inch gauge roads in the world. Many of their officials are friends of mine, including the mechanical engineer I fished with in Nova Scotia.

It was only three months in the hospital that kept me from keeping my date to go down there and I hope that I will soon be able to make up for this great oversight in *Railroading Around the World*. I confidently feel that this is the only great railroad that I have missed inspecting and riding.

New 29 Class 2-8-2 type locomotive hauling crack passenger train at the Rift Valley Escarpment. Twenty of these locomotives were built in Great Britain. They burn oil and are in use on the Kenya and Ugandi section of the road. They can also be readily converted to 3 foot 6 inch gauge if desired and also to vacuum-brake operation. They have a tractive force of 29,835 pounds with 200-pound boiler pressure and 4-foot driving wheels, as the British say (they also call them coupled wheels). Steam brakes have been provided on this engine and Westinghouse air brakes on the tender for train operation. An air-operated valve applies the steam brake when a Westinghouse brake application is made. Westinghouse brake equipment includes two 10 inch by 10½ inch air compressors, a #4 driver's brake application valve with equalizing reservoir, and the usual fittings. The engine is also equipped with a hand brake. The tank carries 4,000 gallons of water and 2,375 gallons of fuel, both imperial gallons. The locomotive is rated for 576 tons on the 1.18 per cent grade, 450 tons on the 1.50 per cent and 352 on the 2.0 per cent grades. On these grades the oil fuel consumption is figured at 7 gallons per mile.

Line-up of Garrett locomotives at Nairobi locomotive shed. Thirty-four of these Garretts of completely new design are in service. They weigh 240 tons and are the heaviest locomotives ever to operate on a meter gauge railway and are 60 tons heavier than the largest locomotive in service on the British railways.

The Garretts have a tractive effort of 46,100 pounds and 220-pound boiler pressure. They have 4 cylinders, 16 by 26 inches, and their driving wheel diameter is 54 inches. Grate area is 48.5 square feet. Weight on the driving wheel is 210,560 pounds with total engine weight of 417,200 pounds. The tender carries 6,000 gallons of water and 2,375 gallons of fuel oil, imperial gallons.

The author has ridden quite a few Garretts and has been on many roads that own them and he has never seen more of any one type of locomotive in storage and out of service. They steam poorly, do not get anywhere near their rated horsepower or speed, and are exceedingly hard to keep water in. The only exception he can think of where there has been good performance is on the east side of the Andes on the Transandine section of the General San Martin Railroad in the Argentine, where they are bucking 6 per cent grades on a rack and do not have to make speed or any time. None have ever been in service in North America.

Philippine Islands

THE railroads in the Philippines, as might be surmised, have recovered slowly from what they have been through in World War II. Much of their recovery so far must be credited to the Luzon Military Railroad and its organization, which went into operation in January, 1945, right after American forces invaded Luzon. This railroad was operated during 1945 by Colonel Frank E. Russell, now Superintendent of Motive Power of the Southern Pacific at Houston, Texas, and a great job was done in restoring operations during that time. The author was in and out of the Philippines for about six weeks in 1945 and went all around the railroad several times. As there was a chapter on this in *Railroading from the Rear End*, we will not go into it further here.

Colonel Frank E. Russell and the author, in front of Colonel Russell's business car, formerly President Quezon's private car. Notice the dwarf business car porter. He really can make up those upper berths!

This is Mrs. S. Kip Farrington Jr.'s pass on the Luzon Military Railroad in 1945.

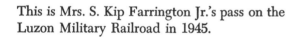

Colonel Frank E. Russell stands in front of 350-horsepower diesel which hauled a special train operated for the author so that he could see the entire railroad operation on the Island of Luzon. The engine and train crew slept in the box car behind the diesel.

Japan

THE Japanese National Railways are remarkably good. Since its first 18 miles of track were put into service in 1872, this railroad has developed into the largest railroad in the Orient. The railroad operates 13,000 miles, or 19,700 kilometers, of track, an annual transportation of 28,000,000,000 ton-kilometers and 64,000,000,000 passenger-kilometers. There are 1,016 miles of electrification. There are 5,336 steam locomotives and 358 electric locomotives, 108,000-odd freight cars, and 11,000 passenger cars, plus 37 ferry boats. The railroad will carry 3 billion people in a year and think nothing of it. Half a million people are employed by the railroad.

Even during the severest air raids in the Pacific war, trains were operated as calmly as in peacetime by civilian railroad men with high efficiency so far as it was physically possible. Years of poor maintenance during the war, and abnormal social and economic conditions after the war, naturally affected Japan's postwar operations. In December, 1948, the Japanese Diet passed the bill to establish a public corporation to operate the whole system of government railways. A new corporation came into existence on June 1, 1949, taking over the entire system of the Japanese Government Railroads under the name of the Japanese National Railways. The new outfit is doing a good job.

The Japanese have two crack passenger trains—the Subame Limited (*Subame* means "Swallow") between Tokyo and Osaki, a 12-hour trip which has just been shortened 3 hours, and the Hato Limited (*Hato* means "Pigeon"). They have regular observation cars and parlor cars somewhat similar to those of the United States. Their sleeping cars have berths like the old U. S. sleepers—I do not know whether this is much to recommend them. When I say berths I mean the open-section type of car. They also have excellent dining cars with seating for two and four and serve very good food. Their coaches are also American style. They have a good many roller bearings on their cars and all of the through-line service cars are equipped with them. They have only about one British practice left and that is left-hand running and left-hand operation of their locomotives. Their road has gone completely to the United States couplers—all of their cars having been converted many years ago—and they have a modern car-washing plant like the United States at the Shinagawa Coach Yard at Tokyo. Their suburban traffic is enormous and they have first-class seats on their multiple-unit trains giving excellent service.

The most impressive thing the Japanese have is a modern hump yard with retarders, and this yard is good for the classification of 7,000 cars a day. It is a

12-cylinder hump retarder. (Japan, Switzerland, Chile, and France are the only places I know of where retarders are in service outside the United States.) Their locomotives are completely equipped with Westinghouse air brake systems. As with the Chileans, the majority of their freight cars are of steel construction, and they are "bogie," as the British say, consisting of two 4-wheel trucks, not the small 4-wheel wagons so popular in Europe. Stations are kept in fine shape, amazingly neat, and their freight houses are built for good operation. There is also much ferry business between the islands. A 4-wheel wagon box car in Japan carries 15 metric tons; with two 4-wheel trucks this car would take 25 tons. Their tank cars have 30 metric ton capacity. Their hopper cars take 30 metric tons. Their gondolas take 35 and their largest box cars take 30. I am listing these figures to show the difference between 4-wheel wagons and the U. S. type of freight car.

Nine million passengers a day will use this railroad and their train miles run over 400,000. They have 100-pound rail on the main lines and their interlockings, ballast, and track are amazingly good. They operate the world's longest undersea tunnel, between Shimonoseki and Moji, connecting two islands. A Japanese train dispatcher will handle over 20 trains per hour in a rush hour and the American dispatching system is in vogue. Their communications and signaling are exceptionally good; for instance, their automatic exchange unit in Tokyo has 2,100 circuits and their exchange boards for toll calls have 1,300 circuits. The line between Tokyo and Osaki is completely electrified and the speed limit is 100 kilometers per hour.

The heavy main-line passenger service on the Japanese National Railways is hauled by their Class C-62 4-6-4 type passenger locomotive. This locomotive has a tractive effort of 30,600 pounds, has 68-inch wheels and 227 pounds boiler pressure. The weight on the driving wheels is only 107,145 pounds and the total engine only weighs 191,500 pounds, but it does the job and is a nice piece of motive power. Before that, and still in service, is the Japanese C-59 4-6-2 type passenger locomotive with the same size driving wheels and the same tractive effort. The other engine, of course, will roll the train much faster with more tonnage.

As elsewhere, the railroads are handicapped by the size of their tenders. The tanks on both of the locomotives described above take only 5,280 gallons of water and 9.85 tons of coal.

For freight service the Japanese have a small but able 2-8-2 type Class D-51 locomotive. This locomotive has 55-inch driving wheels, weight on the drivers of 123,400 pounds, total engine weight of 169,000 pounds, and a tractive force of 37,400 pounds. Weakness in bridges and culverts, I understand, keeps the Japanese from getting bigger motive power, and their clearances are also not what they might be. This locomotive takes only 4,400 gallons and 7.9 tons of coal in its tank. It is equipped with Westinghouse air brakes and an 8½-inch cross compound pump, as is the C-62 Class.

There are not many private railroads or small lines in Japan as there are in Germany and so many other countries.

The Japanese use a good deal of stone ballast and rails are welded in most of the tunnels. Their main line curvature is not too bad—in fact, there is not much worse than 10 degrees on the whole railroad but on a few branch lines it runs up to 17 degrees. Their steepest grades are 2.5 per cent on the main lines and 3.5 per cent on the branch lines.

The longest Japanese bridge is 4,040 feet and their longest double-track bridge is 3,971 feet. They have 10 bridges for a length of 2,595 feet or more, one carrying four tracks. But they really have the tunnels! There are 2,665 of them with a total length of 815,753 meters. The longest tunnel is the Shimizu, which is 31,870 feet long and was built for the purpose of connecting Kento with Niigata by rail. It took nine years to build and is electrified. It is in reality a loop system of six tunnels besides the main one. The heaviest grade in the tunnel is 1.52. The Usuti Tunnels between Maruiama and Yakasaki signal stations on the Shinetsu main line are remarkable, with an elevation at one end of 424 meters and at the other end of 940 meters. The twenty-six tunnels total 4,070 meters in length and the grade is 5 per cent. The tunnel is electrified. The series of Kamon Tunnels on the island of Honshu is also very interesting, having 2 per cent grades and a length of 3,600 meters. The underwater portion of the No. 1 tunnel is approximately 1,600 meters long. This tunnel is 530 kilometers from Kobi on the Sano line.

Yes, aided by the American railway battalions in Japan during the occupation, the Japanese have done a great job and they have taken much good United States advice. Besides that, they are terrific workers. My experience in Japan has been extremely limited and I was there at a very sad time for them, October, 1945. But even at that early date, six weeks after the Armistice was signed, they were hard at work putting the railroads back in order and repairing the damage, and were already much ahead of the Philippines which had been liberated at an earlier date. When I was in Japan at that time, I was sent by the Navy for the express purpose of seeing the railroads, but I must say that when I arrived I was more interested in finding a place to sleep than I was in looking at the railroads. However, I did spend some time around Tokyo in the stations and shops and at Yokosuka, where I had an excellent berth on a big American battleship while there, and I did manage to ride from Tokyo to Osaka, and even at that time was greatly impressed. For my information on the Japanese National Railways, I am indebted to my good friend Colonel Gene M. Gray, who was Director of Operations there in 1950, and who is a great all-around railroader off the Norfolk & Western. He lives in Roanoke, that Norfolk & Western town between the Blue Ridge and the Alleghenies, so many miles from Tokyo.

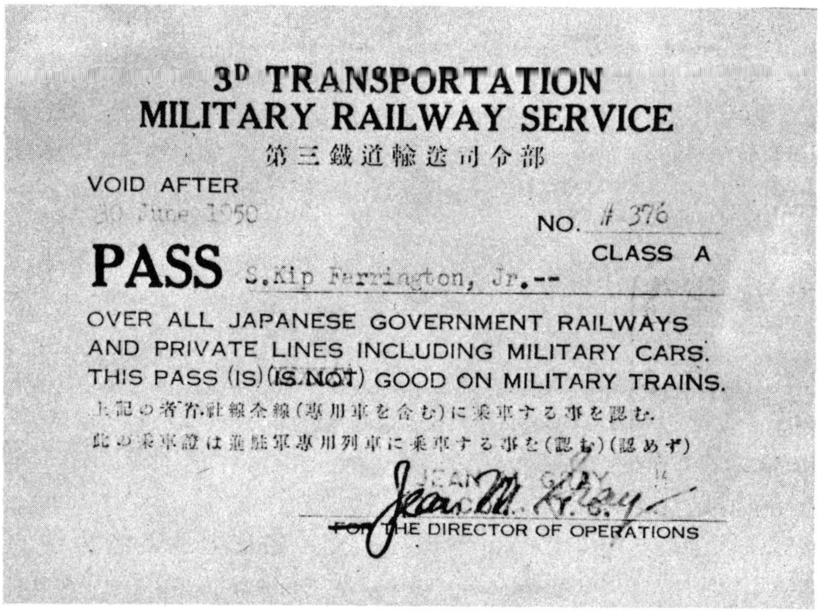

**3ᴰ TRANSPORTATION
MILITARY RAILWAY SERVICE**

第三鐵道輸送司令部

VOID AFTER

30 June 1950

NO. # 376

PASS S.Kip Farrington, Jr.--

CLASS A

OVER ALL JAPANESE GOVERNMENT RAILWAYS
AND PRIVATE LINES INCLUDING MILITARY CARS.
THIS PASS (IS) (IS NOT) GOOD ON MILITARY TRAINS.

上記の者右社線全線(專用車を含む)に乘車する事を認む.

此の乘車證は進駐軍専用列車に乘車する事を(認む)(認めず)

Jean M. Gray

THE DIRECTOR OF OPERATIONS

Author's pass on the Military Railway Service in Japan, signed
by Lieutenant Colonel Gene M. Gray, who was director of operations. Colonel Gray is off the Norfolk & Western, is from Roanoke,
Virginia, and is a fine all-around railroader.

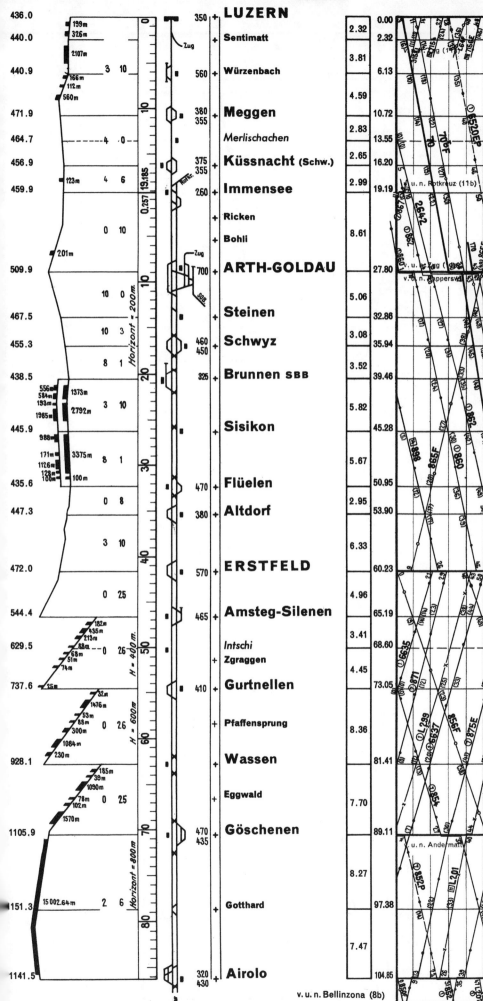

Swiss operating timetable, with profile, showing tunnels on the Gotthard Line, their lengths, altitudes, distances between stations, stations, tracks and sidings. This is typical of train graphs used on so many of the world's railroads. Each line represents a train movement. Note spiral tunnels.

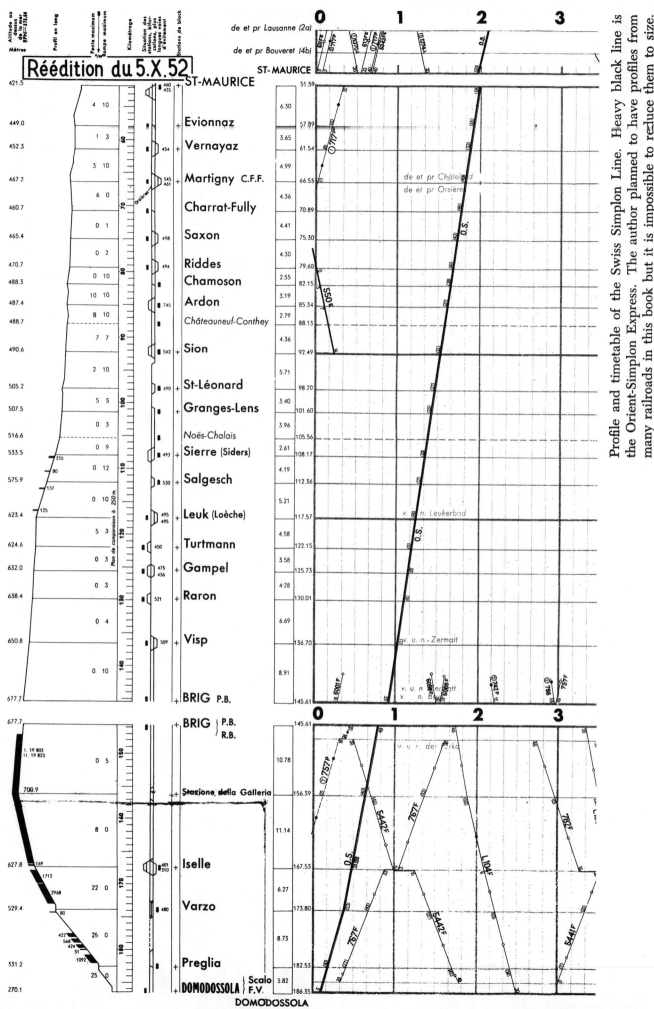

Profile and timetable of the Swiss Simplon Line. Heavy black line is the Orient-Simplon Express. The author planned to have profiles from many railroads in this book but it is impossible to reduce them to size.

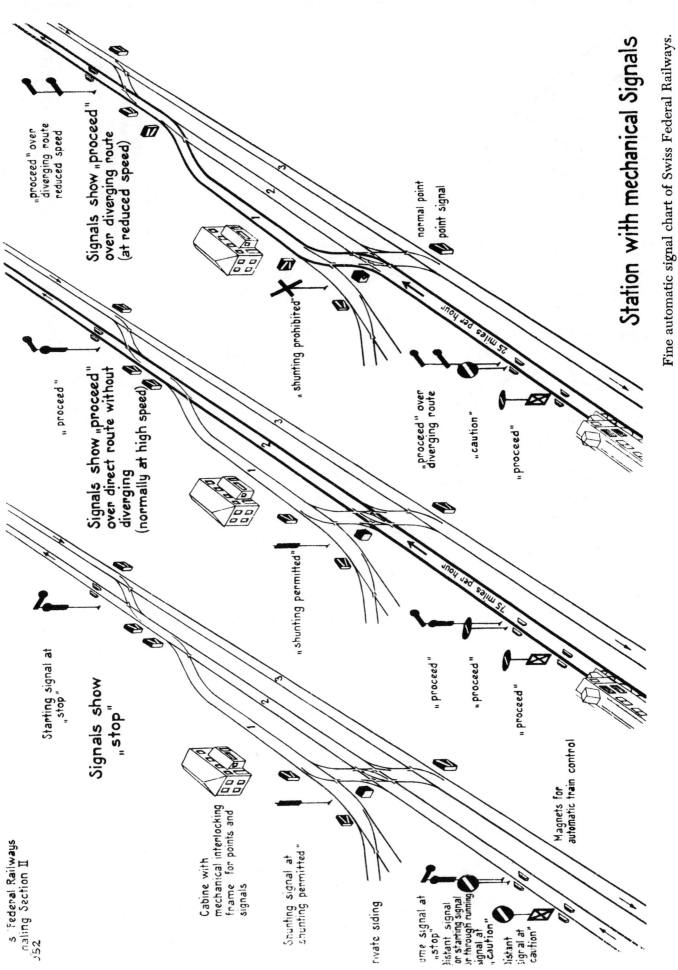

Station with mechanical Signals

Fine automatic signal chart of Swiss Federal Railways.

Labels within the figure:

"proceed" over diverging route reduced speed

Signals show "proceed" over diverging route (at reduced speed)

normal point point signal

"proceed" over diverging route

"caution"

"proceed"

"shunting prohibited"

25 miles per hour

"proceed"

Signals show "proceed" over direct route without diverging (normally at high speed)

"shunting permitted"

75 miles per hour

"proceed"

"proceed"

"proceed"

"proceed"

Magnets for automatic train control

Starting signal at "stop"

Signals show "stop"

Cabine with mechanical interlocking frame for points and signals

Shunting signal at "shunting permitted"

Private siding

Home signal at "stop"

Distant signal or starting signal or through running signal at "Caution"

Distant signal at "caution"

s Federal Railways naling Section II 552

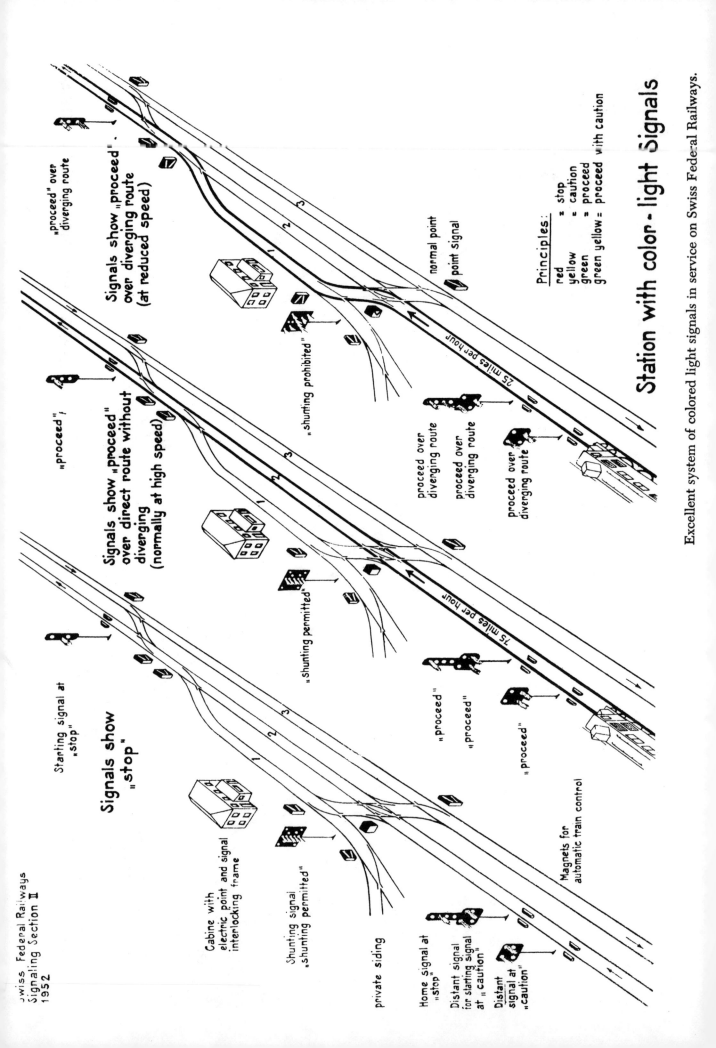

Swiss Federal Railways
Signaling Section II
1952

Starting signal at "stop"

Signals show "stop"

Cabine with electric point and signal interlocking frame

Shunting signal "shunting permitted"

private siding

Home signal at "stop"

Distant signal for starting signal at "caution"

Distant signal at "caution"

"proceed"

Signals show "proceed" over direct route without diverging (normally at high speed)

"shunting permitted"

75 miles per hour

"proceed"

"proceed"

"proceed"

Magnets for automatic train control

"proceed" over diverging route

Signals show "proceed" over diverging route (at reduced speed)

"shunting prohibited"

normal point

point signal

25 miles per hour

proceed over diverging route

proceed over diverging route

proceed over diverging route

Principles:
red = stop
yellow = caution
green = proceed
green yellow = proceed with caution

Station with color-light Signals

Excellent system of colored light signals in service on Swiss Federal Railways.

THE AUTOMATIC SAFETY – INSTALLATION FOR TRAINS.

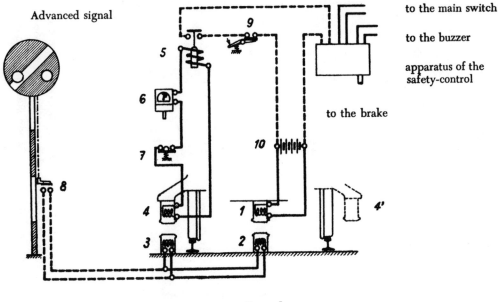

Advanced signal

to the main switch

to the buzzer

apparatus of the safety-control

to the brake

Legend:

1 Exciting magnet
2 Inside rail-magnet
3 Outside rail-magnet
4 & 4' Receiving magnets
5 Relay of the automatic safety-installation

6 Tachometer
7 Release-key
8 Contact on the advanced signal
9 Pedal-switch
10 Battery

Automatic train control system used on Swiss Federal Railways.

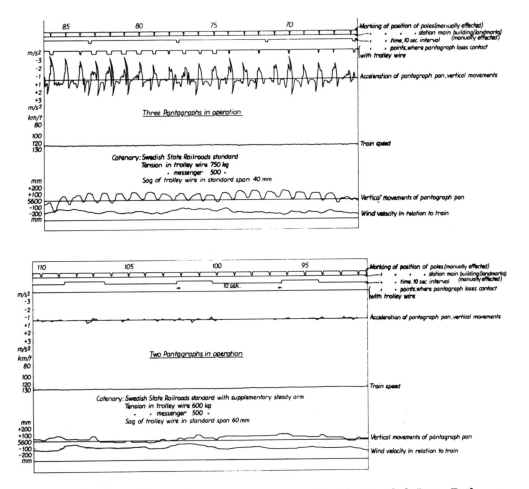

Graph taken from electric dynamometer car used by the Swedish State Railways showing pantograph action.

Fortsettelse fra foregående side.

Avst.	Stasjoner m.v.	Inn Spor	Spor	Til	Opphold	Fra	Ut	Krysser	Kjører(es) forbi
	Voss	O	1	18.55	15	19.10		{ 1844 / 5516 }	615
8.06	Bulken		1			21			
10.28	Evanger		2			32		616	
10.47	Bolstadøyri		2			44		600	
11.16	Dale		1			20.01			
6.93	Stanghelle	↳	2			08			
8.31	Vaksdal		2			17			
11.88	Trengereid		2			31			
10.72	Garnes		1			44		606	
3.66	Arna		1			49			
7.50	Haukeland		2[1]			21.01		1812	
8.25	Nesttun	⊙⊙	1	21.11	3	14	⊙⊙	668	669
1.58	Hop	⊙⊙	1			17	⊙⊙		
2.21	Fjøsanger	⊙⊙	1			20	⊙⊙		
1.93	Minde	⊙⊙	2			23	⊙⊙	670	
1.37	Kronstad	⊙⊙	1			26	⊙⊙		
2.67	Bergen	⊙	1	21.30					

[1] *Helligdager* spor 1

Norwegian State Railways operating timetable, showing page for each train. "S" inserted by author riding locomotive is for snow-shed, "T" for tunnel. Shown are distances between stations, signals, number of tracks, arrival and departure times at stations, meets and passes.

Alle dager 1. juni—3. oktober, ellers bare søndager, tirsdager og torsdager.

2. og 3. kl. Luftbr. Aks. 68. Sth. 70. Tlf.

Avst.	Stasjoner m.v.	Inn Spor	Spor	Til	Opphold	Fra	Ut	Krysser	Kjører(es) forbi
	Oslo Ø.					9.35			
10.88	Hønefoss			*11.30*	15	11.45			5531
11.54	Veme		1			12.01		1824	
8.61	Sokna		1		■	16			
7.68	Rallerud		1		■	27			
12.50	Ørgenvika	⊙⊙	2		△	37		5532	
11.22	Gulsvik		1		■	51			
7.87	Flå		1		■	13.05			
13.90	Austvoll		1		■	15			
11.65	Bromma		2		■	32			
16.96	Nesbyen	⊙⊙	1	13.45	5	50			
15.47	Gol		1	14.07	5	14.12			
10.36	Torpo		1	31	4	35		602	
13.34	Ål	O	1	53	15	15.08		{ 5512 / 5534 }	5511
11.19	Hol	O	1	15.28	2	30		610	
11.93	Geilo		1	48	3	51			
10.83	Ustaoset		1	16.11	2	16.13		5514	
13.20	Haugastøl		1	25	5	30			
13.40	Tunga		2		▲	45			
20.70	Finse	O	1	17.00	10	17.10			
13.00	Hallingskeid	O	1			54			
6.35	Myrdal		1	47		18.01			
12.07	Upsete								
8.51	Mjølfjell		1		■	15			
8.79	Reimegrend		1		■	26			
7.51	Urdland		1		■	37			
6.29	Ygre		1			47			
	Voss	O	1	18.55	15	19.10		{ 1844 / 5516 }	615

FERROCARRIL CENTRAL DEL PERU

ORDEN TELEGRAFICA DE TREN No.

Recibido de.............el...........de...............de 194......

TIP "EL FERROCARRIL"

A.. EN..................................

.... Tel...............................

Recibido a las..............M.   Repetida a las..............M.

CONDUCTOR	MAQUINISTA	TREN	HECHA	HORA	TELEGRAFISTA

NOTA:—Conductor y Maquinista deben recabar copia de orden Reclame sus copias de Ordenes de Precaución.

T. 31 B. D.

FERROCARRIL CENTRAL DEL PERU

SOLAMENTE PARA ESTACIONES DE REGISTRO

Boleta Despachador No.............

.... Estación   194............

Conductor y Maquinista Tren..................................

Las Ordenes para Ud. son Nos ....

(Si no hay órdenes, escriba "Ninguna" en la primera línea prevista para los Nos de las Ordenes).

FIRMAS		HORA COMPLETA	FIRMA TELEGRAFISTA
CONDUCTOR	MAQUINISTA		

Ningún tren saldrá de una estación de Registro, sin tener esta forma.
Esta no anula, ni modifica, ninguna Orden que haya Ud. recibido.
Conductor y Maquinista deben tener cada uno, una copia de esta Boleta cerciorándose, que los Nos. de las Ordenes, que reciban estén anotadas correctamente.
Los Telegrafistas guardarán una copia.

Hora Salida.................................

Central Railroad of Peru's train order receipt.

Thirty-one order in Spanish used on Central R.R. of Peru. One of the few railroads that uses train orders outside of North America.

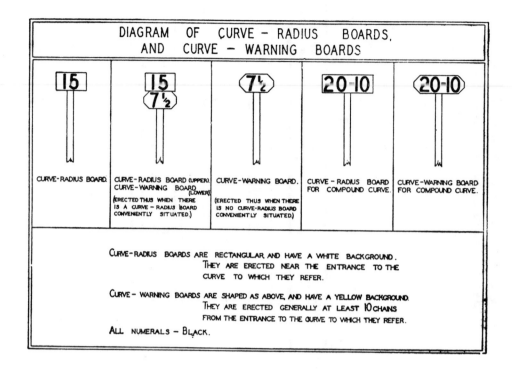

Curve-radius boards in service on New Zealand Government Railways.

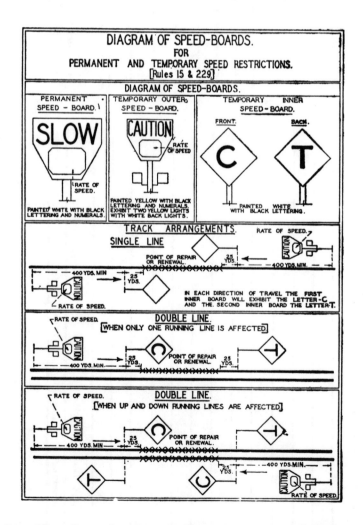

Speed boards used on New Zealand Government Railways.

Form Mis. 21

N.Z.R.   *Mis. 21.*

TABLET INSTRUMENT OUT OF ORDER.

No................

...............,.............19 .

Train No.......................

From.......................

To ....

Officer in Charge.

NEW ZEALAND GOVERNMENT RAILWAYS.   *Mis. 21.*

ELECTRIC TRAIN TABLET SYSTEM.

TABLET INSTRUMENT OUT OF ORDER.

No................

To Engine-driver of Train No............... Date...............

Tablet working not being in operation between ....
and ...., I have obtained " Line Clear," as shown in the attached telegram, for Train No..............., which is hereby authorized to proceed from...............to.................

Officer in Charge.

Form Mis. 28

N.Z.R.   *Mis. 28.*

TRAIN STAFF TICKET.

No................

...............,.............19 .

Train No.......................

From.......................

To ....

Officer in Charge.

NEW ZEALAND GOVERNMENT RAILWAYS.   *Mis. 28.*

TRAIN STAFF TICKET.

No. .... *Station.*

To Engine-driver of Train No............... Date...............

You are authorized, after seeing the Train Staff for the Section, to proceed from...............to...............and the Train Staff will follow.

Previous train left at.................

Officer in Charge.

Form Mis. 46

N.Z.R.   *Mis. 46.*

...............,.............19 .

Officer in Charge.

Received Certificate stating that...............Station is switched in / switched out for my train, which is authorized to travel to...............Station only, as per tablet received.

Engine-driver.

Train No.......... ....19 .

NEW ZEALAND GOVERNMENT RAILWAYS.   *Mis. 46.*

ELECTRIC TRAIN TABLET SYSTEM.

ALTERATION OF TABLET ARRANGEMENTS— SWITCH-OUT STATIONS.

...............19 .

To Engine-driver of Train No............... Date.................

...............Station is* switched in / switched out for your train, which* will / will not be signalled there. Your attention is drawn to the tablet now handed to you, which authorizes Train No...............to run to...............Station.

(* Delete words not required.)   *Officer in Charge.*

Form Mis. 52

N.Z.R.   *Mis. 52.*

WRONG-LINE ORDER.

No................

...............19 .

Authorizing Train No...............
to return to this signal-box on the wrong line, due to ....
....
....

Signalman.

NEW ZEALAND GOVERNMENT RAILWAYS.   *Mis. 52.*

AUTOMATIC SIGNALLING — WRONG-LINE ORDER.

No................

...............19 .

To Engine-driver of Train No............... Date.................
I hereby authorise Train No............... to return on the Wrong Line to the signal-box at...............
Catch points exist at...............
(Delete, if no catch point exist.)

Signalman.

Countersigned :

Engine-driver.   Guard.   Following Train No.

....

Various ticket forms used in operation of New Zealand Government Railways.

SINGLE-LINE AUTOMATIC SIGNALLING.
CROSSING ORDER.

Crossing order No. ..		Sent at	
Office of origin		Sent by	
Date	19	Repeated back by	, from
Time	a.m. p.m.	", ", at	a.m. p.m.

To Engine-driver and Guard,

Train No......, at.......

To-day,........ No........ will cross No........ at.......

Instructions: ....

NOTE.—This does not authorize the passing of Departure signals at "**Stop**".

.................., Dist. Traffic Mgr.   Per........   Train Control Operator.

SINGLE-LINE AUTOMATIC SIGNALLING.
Authority to Pass Departure Signal in the Stop Position.

Authority No. ..		Sent at.. ..	
Office of Origin ..		", by.. ..	
Date	/ 194	Repeated back by	
Time	a.m. p.m.	", , from ", at	a.m. p.m.

To Engine-driver and Guard,

Train No......, at.......

To-day,........ No........ is authorized to pass the........

DEPARTURE signal at........ in the Stop position.

.................., Dist. Traffic Mgr., per........   Train Control Operator.

SINGLE-LINE AUTOMATIC SIGNALLING.
CROSSING ORDER.

To be filled in on copy retained in book.

Crossing order No. ..		Received at ..	
Office of origin ..		; by ..	
Date	19	Repeated back by ..	
Time	a.m. p.m.	", ", at ..	a.m. p.m.

To Engine-driver and Guard,

Train No......, at.......

To-day,........ No........ will cross No........ at.......

Instructions: ....

NOTE.—This does not authorize the passing of Departure signals at "**Stop**".

.................., Dist. Traffic Mgr.

SINGLE-LINE AUTOMATIC SIGNALLING.
Authority to Pass Departure Signal in the Stop Position:

Authority No. ..	
Office of Origin ..	
Date	/ 194
Time	a.m. p.m.

To Engine-driver and Guard,

Train No......, at.......

To-day,........ No........ is authorized to pass the........ in the Stop position.

DEPARTURE signal at........

NOTE.—The train must travel cautiously, the engine-driver being prepared to find the section obstructed, points wrongly set, or a broken or misplaced rail.
The engine headlamp must be lighted when passing through tunnels or when visibility is bad.

Countersigned,........

Guard, No........ Train........   District Traffic Manager.

Crossing or "meeting" forms (*left*) and permissive tickets (*right*) used on New Zealand Government Railways, signed by Traffic Manager (Superintendent) or Train Control Operator (Dispatcher).

Tyer's Automatic Tablet Apparatus
— with —
— Visual Signals —

Visual Indications.

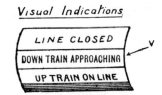

Screen Enlarged.

Bell & Relay.

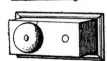

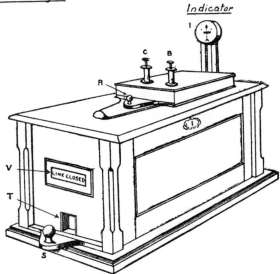

CODE OF BELL SIGNALS FOR TABLET-WORKING.

See Reg.	Signal.	No. of Beats.	How to be given.
1	Speak on Telephone	1	1.
3 and 4	Is line clear for Ordinary Passenger Train ..	4	4, consecutively.
	" *Fast Train	4	2, pause, 2.
	" Mixed Train	5	5, consecutively.
	" Empty Carriage Train ..	5	2, pause, 2, pause, /.
	" Goods Train or Engine and Brake	6	6, consecutively.
	" Work-train	6	3, pause, 3.
	" Light Engine	6	2, pause, 2, pause, 2.
	" Train or Engine entering Section to return to starting-point	6	3, pause, 2, pause, 1.
5	Departure Signal for any class of Train ..	2	2, consecutively.
6	Arrival " " ..	3	3, consecutively.

* Mail or Express Trains or any that may be shown as "Fast" in Ordinary or Special Time tables, also Casualty Vans or Relief Engines, are to be so Signalled.

New Zealand Government Railways tablet apparatus with bell signals for tablet working.

N.Z.R.   Mis. 29.
PILOTMAN'S TICKET.

No.............................

........................., ...19

Train No......................

From..............................

To..............................

Preceding train No......................

has arrived at..............................

left at............... a.m.
.... p.m.

....
Pilotman.

NEW ZEALAND GOVERNMENT RAILWAYS.   Mis. 29.
PILOT WORKING — PILOTMAN'S TICKET.

No..............................

..............................19 .

To Engine-driver of Train No.................. Date..............................
Train No.............. is hereby authorized to proceed from ....
to ...., Pilotman following.
The preceding train (No..............)* has arrived at..............................
left at.............. a.m.
.... p.m.

(*Delete words not required.)   ....
Pilotman.

N.Z.R.   Mis. 31.
No......................

........................., ...19 .

....
Officer in Charge.

Received Ticket, numbered as above, stating that the Signal Adjuster or Maintainer is examining machines at.........................., which place must be approached cautiously.

....
Engine-driver.

Train No.......... ....19 .

NEW ZEALAND GOVERNMENT RAILWAYS.   Mis. 31.
SIGNAL STAFF WORKING ON SECTION.

No..............................

..............................19 .

To Engine-driver of Train No.................. Date..............................
The Signal Adjuster or Maintainer is on the section examining the machines at..............................Siding, for which purpose he may use the facing points; you must therefore approach the Siding with care and have your train under control, so as to be able to stop short of the facing points at such Siding should any hand signal be given for that purpose.

....
Officer in Charge.

NEW ZEALAND GOVERNMENT RAILWAYS.   Mis. 39.
TRAIN STOPPED IN SECTION.

..............................19

a.m.
p.m.

To the Signalman at.........................., and Engine-driver of Relief Train or Engine.
My train has stopped in the section between..............................and.............................., and requires assistance.
I will not move my engine in any direction until the arrival of the Relief Train or Engine.

Countersigned :

....
Guard, Train No................... .

....
Engine-driver, Train No................... .

Catch points exist at.......................... .
(Delete, if no catch points exist.)

NEW ZEALAND GOVERNMENT RAILWAYS.   Mis. 43.
CANCELLING PILOT WORKING.

....

To.........................., ...19 .

a.m.
p.m.

at.......................... .

Pilot working instituted at this station on..............................19 , for the section between..............................
and..............................is hereby cancelled, and ordinary working will now be resumed.

....
Officer in Charge.

Other types of ticket authorization in use in New Zealand.

Mis. 53.

NEW ZEALAND GOVERNMENT RAILWAYS.

AUTOMATIC SIGNALLING.
ESTABLISHING PILOT WORKING ON SINGLE LINE.

From District Traffic Manager,

To.

(Full name and designation.)

You are authorized to have possession of the Pilot Key and act as Pilotman between and in accordance with Regulation No. 28, until further advised.

Time :

Date : District Traffic Manager.

(When this form is cancelled it must be forwarded to the District Traffic Manager.)

NEW ZEALAND GOVERNMENT RAILWAYS.

AUTOMATIC SIGNALLING.
CANCELLING PILOT WORKING ON SINGLE LINE.

From District Traffic Manager,

To.

(Full name and designation.)

Your authority to act as Pilotman between

and is hereby cancelled.

Time :

Date : District Traffic Manager.

Mis. 54.

NEW ZEALAND GOVERNMENT RAILWAYS.

AUTOMATIC SIGNALLING.
PILOT WORKING ON SINGLE LINE—PILOT'S TICKET.

To Driver and Guard of Train No.

After seeing Pilot Key for section you are authorized to proceed from Station to Station,

Pilotman following.

Date : Pilotman.

Mis. 33.

NEW ZEALAND GOVERNMENT RAILWAYS.

INSTITUTING PILOT WORKING.

19 .

a.m.
p.m.

To

at

The *

all traffic will pass between and , who will act as Pilotman.

in the charge of

An engine or train must not be allowed to leave

for or

for

unless the Pilotman is present and gives permission.

This order must remain in force until withdrawn by the Pilotman presenting a Mis. 43 Cancellation form signed by the Officer in Charge for the time being at this station.

Officer in Charge.

Catch points exist at.
(Delete, if no catch points exist.)

Noted by†	at	a.m. / p.m.
Noted by†	at	a.m. / p.m.
Noted by†	at	a.m. / p.m.
Noted by†	at	a.m. / p.m.
Noted by†	at	a.m. / p.m.
Noted by†	at	a.m. / p.m.
Noted by†	at	a.m. / p.m.
Noted by†	at	a.m. / p.m.
Noted by†	, Pilotman.	a.m. / p.m.

* Here insert "Line being blocked at between and ," or "Tablet
(or Staff) for the section between and having been lost," or
"Communication having failed," or as the case may be.

† These signatures must be made on the copy held by the Pilotman.

Pilot tickets as used by New Zealand Government Railways and other English-speaking railroads.

N.Z.R. MINIMUM STANDARD CLEARANCES.
1930.

THE CLEARANCES SHOWN ARE THE MINIMUM STANDARD CLEARANCES. CLEARANCES THAT ENCROACH ON THE MINIMUM ARE SPECIALLY NOTIFIED TO STAFF WHEN NECESSARY.

THE EXTREME DIMENSIONS OF LOAD PERMITTED EXCEPT IN SUCH CASES AS MAY BE SPECIALLY AUTHORIZED ARE:—

HEIGHT ABOVE RAIL LEVEL	WIDTH EACH SIDE OF CENTRE OF TRACK
FROM RAIL TO 10 FEET	4 FEET
FROM 10 FT. TO 11 FT. 6 IN.	TAPERING FROM 4 FT. TO 2 FT. 6 IN.

THE EXTREME HEIGHT IS 11 FT. 6 IN.
THE EXTREME WIDTH IS 4 FT. FROM CENTRE LINE OF TRACK

LINING

TUNNEL

OVERBRIDGES

VERANDAH EAVES

GOODS SHED AND ENGINE SHED DOORS

EXTREME DIMENSIONS OF LOADS

GOODS SHED AND ENGINE SHED DOORS

SHEEP AND CATTLE YARDS

BRIDGE TRUSSES, TANK STANDS, SIGNALS, TABLET EXCHANGERS, BUILDINGS FROM SIDINGS, AND LIMIT OF MATERIAL STACKING FROM SIDINGS

OVERBRIDGE PIERS

LIMIT OF STACKING MATERIALS FROM MAIN LINE

BUILDING FROM MAIN LINE

PLATFORM VERANDAH POSTS

LEVEL

CENTRE LINE OF TRACK

FLOORS OF WAGONS

COAL BINS AT COLLIERIES

EXTREME HEIGHT OF LOAD

ENGINE SMOKE TROUGHS

GOODS SHED AND ENGINE SHED DOORS

OVERBRIDGES 14' 3" (14' 6" IN SUBURBAN AREAS)

RAIL

SIDINGS WITH GOODS SHEDS

SPECIAL PLATFORMS

ORDINARY PLATFORMS

SHEEP & CATTLE YARD RAMP LOADING BANKS

GOODS SHED PLATFORMS SPECIAL AND VERANDAH

ORDINARY 3'0" & 4'6" THROUGH

LOADING BANKS AND GOODS SHED PLATFORM

SHEEP AND CATTLE RAMPS

SIDINGS FROM SIDINGS

SIDINGS FROM MAIN LINE

4' 0"
5' 0"
6' 0"
6' 9"
7' 0"
8' 0"
9' 0"
11' 0"
2' 6"
4' 0"
9' 0"
9' 6"
10' 0"
11' 6"
11' 7"
12' 0"
15' 0"
12' 0"
11' 0"
3' 6½"
2' 9¾" TO 3' 0"
3' 2"
2' 6"
2' 8"

Standard clearances on New Zealand Government 3 foot 6 inch gauge railroad.

English Railroad Terms

As Used in British Empire, India, Australia, New Zealand, and Some of the Spanish-, German-, and French-Speaking Countries.

British	U. S.	British	U. S.
Signal box	Tower or signal station	Collieries	Coal mines
		Train examiner	Car inspector
Breakdown vans	Wrecking trains	Line clear ticket	Ticket type of clearance cards
Break vans	Caboose		
Locomotive shed	Engine terminal	Pilot man	Individual who rides trains or locomotives without a staff or ticket in staff territory
Locomotive shed master	Enginehouse foreman		
Goods trains	Freight trains		
Wagons	Freight cars		
Vehicles	Passenger cars		
Axles	Number of axles in the train	Mail sorting van	Our P.O. car
		Line side	Along the right-of-way
Bogies	Four-wheel trucks		
Foot plate	Deck of locomotive	Mail pick-up standards	Mail cranes
Driver	Engineman	Draw gear	Drawheads
Regulator	Throttle	Guard	Conductor
Assistant locomotive	Helper	Brake sticks	Brake club
Banker	Pusher	Express goods	Fast freight
Cross	Meet	Empty coaching stock	Deadhead equipment
Loop	Passing track	Reception line	Inbound yard track
Level crossing	Highway crossing	Performing trains	Making up trains
Shunter	Yard or switch engine	Attaching vehicles	Picking up cars
Shunting	Switching	Brake cars	Express cars
Marshall yard	Freight yard	Ambulance boxes	First-aid kits
Marshalling	Classifying	Crow	Peep of the engine steam whistle
Engine road	Engine track to engine house		
		Sleepers	Ties
Coaling road	Coal track	Permanent way inspector	Roadmaster
Sorting sidings	Classification tracks		
Reception sidings	Receiving yards	Fog signalman	A permanent wayman who is picked as f o g signalman and put at fogging posts where signals cannot be seen during fog or falling snow
Assembling sidings	Departure sidings		
Neck	Throat		
Double incline	Hump		
Down yard shunting ⎫	Switching tracks up or down to the yard		
Up yard shunting ⎭			
Downtrain	From the home terminal	Work rumpus	Work gang

223

British	U. S.	British	U. S.
Uptrain	To the home terminal	Bank	Grade
Hours and minutes of departure from home terminal are usually used for down and up trains and not the engine numbers or train numbers			Grades are kept: 1 in 100 — 1%; 1 in 50 — 2%; 1 in 33 — 3%; 1 in 18 — 4%
		In England there are no headlights or bells on locomotives	
Stacking	Coal piles		
Yard controllers	Yardmasters	Goods van	Car that the conductor rides in
Shunting master	Switching foreman, sometimes hump foreman	Wrong line	Running against the current of traffic
Main	Through tracks or main line	Train is divided	Break in two
		Tail lamp	Used instead of marker lamp
Workshops	Shops		
Detonators	Torpedoes (no fuses are used)	Dead end bay	Stub station

Standard Code of Engine Headlamps

Unless otherwise shown in sectional appendices, all engines must carry headlamps or white disks as follows:

1. Two lights or disks on pilot beam—express passenger train or breakdown van going to clear the line or light engine going to assist disabled train.

2. One light under the stack on smokebox—local passenger train, or stopping passenger train, as they call it.

3. One light on pilot beam and 1 light in center of smokebox on pilot beam—express goods; also authorized empty coaching stock.

4. One light or disk on smokebox under stack and 1 light on right side of pilot beam—express goods or empty coaching stock.

5. One light in center of smokebox and 1 light on left side of pilot beam—express goods.

6. One light under stack on smokebox and 1 light on left side—class A goods. One light on smokebox under stack and 1 light in middle of smokebox and pilot beam—class B goods.

7. One light on pilot beam right side—class C goods or ballast train. One light on left side on pilot beam—class D goods or local freight.

8. One single light on pilot beam in middle of smokebox—light engine or engine with not more than two breakdown attached.

Locomotives also carry numbers on their pilot beams designating the shed to which they belong.

English-Spanish Railroad Dictionary

English	Spanish	English	Spanish
Railroad	Ferrocarril	Proceed	Avante
Locomotive	Locomotora	Coupler	Enganche
Signal	Señal	Switch	Desvío
Track	Vía	Station	Estacíon
Rail	Riél	Arrive	Llegar
Car	Vagón, coche	Leave	Salir
Freight	Carga, mercancía	Departure	La salida
Train	Tren	Arrival	La llegada
Passenger	Pasajero, viajero	Dispatcher	Despachar
Mixed	Mixto	Station-Master	El Jefe
Ticket	Billete	Engineer	Maquinista
Pass	Pase	Fireman	Fogonero
Electric	Eléctrico	Conductor	Revisor
Bridge	Puente	Signalman	Guardavía
Grade	Grado	Junction	Empalme
Curve	Curva	Box	Caja
Tender	El tandem casita	Hot-box	Caja caliente
Caboose	Furgón	Operation	Servicio
Mail	Correo	Steam	Vapor
Wheel	Rueda	Trip	Viaje
Brake	Freno	Machine	La máquina
Air	Aire	Firebox	Hogar
Company	Compañía	Boiler	Caldera
Coal	Carbón	Cylinder	Cilindros
Oil	Petróleo	Cross-over	Cruce
Diesel	Diesel	General Manager	Gerente
Motor	Motor	The Director	Director genera
Stock	Ganado	Timetable	Horario
Order	Orden	Staff	Palo
Clearance	Vía libre	Traffic Manager	Jefe departamento
Red	Rojo	Transportation	Transporte
Yellow	Amarillo	Technician	Técnico
Green	Verde	Section	Sección
Stop	Parar	Tariff	Tarifas
Danger	Peligro	Division	Zona
Caution	Cuidado	Clear	Vía libra

There is also a word you might like to know which is used in Chile and which applies to a good many of us around the world. It is "carrilano," which means a man who likes the rail-roads and takes a big chance once in a while.

Index